CIVIL WAR LONDON

A Military History of London under Charles I and Oliver Cromwell

David Flintham

'This is the Century of the Soldier', Falvio Testir, Poet, 1641

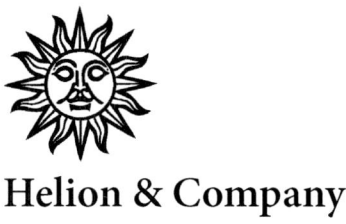

Helion & Company

I would like to dedicate this book to my mother-in-law, Chris Hand,
and to the memory of my father-in-law, Dr. John Hand.

It is also dedicated to the memory of my cousin, Keith Hopkins,
who passed away as this book was nearing completion.

Helion & Company Limited
26 Willow Road
Solihull
West Midlands
B91 1UE
England
Tel. 0121 705 3393
Fax 0121 711 4075
Email: info@helion.co.uk
Website: www.helion.co.uk
Twitter: @helionbooks
Visit our blog at http://blog.helion.co.uk/

Published by Helion & Company 2017
Designed and typeset by Serena Jones
Cover designed by Paul Hewitt, Battlefield Design (www.battlefield-design.co.uk)
Printed by Henry Ling Limited, Dorchester, Dorset

Text © David Flintham 2017
Images open source unless © individually credited

Cover: Based on the painting by Charles West Cope, Steve Noon's front cover depicts the Tower Hamlets Regiment marching to join Waller's army in the summer of 1644, © Helion & Company, 2017

Every reasonable effort has been made to trace copyright holders and to obtain their permission for the use of copyright material. The author and publisher apologize for any errors or omissions in this work, and would be grateful if notified of any corrections that should be incorporated in future reprints or editions of this book.

ISBN 978-1-911512-62-2

British Library Cataloguing-in-Publication Data.
A catalogue record for this book is available from the British Library.

All rights reserved. No part of this publication may be reproduced, stored in a retrieval system, or transmitted, in any form, or by any means, electronic, mechanical, photocopying, recording or otherwise, without the express written consent of Helion & Company Limited.

For details of other military history titles published by Helion & Company
Limited, contact the above address, or visit our website: http://www.helion.co.uk

We always welcome receiving book proposals from prospective authors.

Contents

Preface	4
Introduction	6
1. London in the 1640s	8
2. The Winter Crisis, 1641–42	13
3. The Trained Bands	17
4. A City at War, 1642–46	21
5. London's Armaments Industry	33
6. Counter-Revolution, 1646–49	37
7. The Commonwealth Capital, 1649–58	42
8. The Return of the King, 1658–60	49
The Gazetteer of Civil War London	
Inside the Lines of Communication	52
Outside the Lines of Communication	98
Bibliography	116

Preface

Initially, this book came about as a by-product of two decades of investigation into London's English Civil War fortifications. But once this was published in 2014, I looked again at this research, appreciating that the fortifications represented but one part of London's military involvement in the wars. Several aspects of this have previously been studied, most notably London's militia, the Trained Bands, but this was just one of several armed bodies to grace London's streets during the 1640s and 1650s. It is well known that the Tower of London was the country's greatest arsenal, but less well known is that London had a substantial arms industry, and within London's boundaries could be found military hospitals and military prisons. Many of the conflict's leading soldiers spent time in the capital; some had homes there whilst others found themselves the guest of the Lieutenant of the Tower of London. Thus, London during the 1640s and 50s was very much the militarised city.

But this is just half of the story. As a historian specialising in 17th century fortifications and sieges, I spend as much (if not more) time 'in the field' as I do in archives and libraries: for me the historical landscape is just as important as contemporary accounts and records. In 2010, I was asked by the Royal Geographical Society to devise a walk exploring the English Civil War in Westminster. In researching the route I was surprised by just how many places associated with the period could be found during a 3 mile walk. Inspired by Peter Gaunt's 1987 *The Cromwellian Gazetteer*, I set out to discover just how much of the London known to King Charles I and Oliver Cromwell and their contemporaries can be seen, or at least traced, today. As I discovered, the London of Charles I and Oliver Cromwell was not swept away by the Great Fire, or the Blitz, or by the growth of the capital, and, therefore, deserves as much attention as is given to the London of Shakespeare or Pepys.

In a time when historians of the English Civil War have become preoccupied with the 'causes and meaning of the war', with the result that academic interest in the actual military history of the conflict has declined, I make no excuses for this being a history with a distinct bias to things military. Of course London was politically and economically vital, but this should take nothing away from the impact that the actual fighting had on London and the impact that the capital had on the fighting.

For the sake of clarity, I have used London's 1642–3 fortifications, the 'Lines of Communication', to define London of the 1640s and 50s. Therefore 'London' is the area within the lines, a geographical area stretching from Whitechapel in the east to the edge of Hyde Park in the west, from

PREFACE

Sadler's Wells in the north to St George's Fields in the south, an area which encompassed the City of London itself, plus parts of Westminster, Southwark and the surrounding suburbs. Outside the lines were in the 17th century a number of individual towns and villages, which now fall within modern 'greater London', hence their inclusion within this book.

This book could not have been possible without the help, advice, generosity and encouragement of a great number of people, a number of whom I have had the pleasure to encounter at the various archives, collections and libraries I have used during the course of my research over the years. Some I can thank by name – Alison Lister, Jon Newman, Debbie Smith – but for those whose names I can't recall, I apologise. Their contributions have been no less important.

As a breed, historians are a generous bunch, but even so, I would like to express my gratitude to a number of them who have shared their expertise and research with me, particularly Jane Bowden-Dan, Ross Davies, Serena Jones, Simon Marsh, Stephen Porter, Victoria Ridgeway, and Andrew Robertshaw. Additionally, thanks also go to all my fellow fortress and military historians who have given me so much encouragement, advice and support over the years, in particular: Charles Blackwood, Gilbert Dowdall-Brown, Neil Faulkner, David Harding, Peter Harrington and Michael Osborne.

I am indebted to Anne Thackray for her expertise on all things Wenceslaus Hollar, to Simon Turner for discovering the Hyde Park fort sketch, and to John Shoesmith (University of Toronto), Suzanne Fagan (University of Manchester), and Alan Turton for their generosity in allowing me to use a number of the illustrations.

I would also like to thank Peter Gaunt for his original inspiration, and importantly, I would like to thank Charles Singleton for his interest in this project and for his encouragement, patience, help and expertise throughout the life of this book. Any mistakes are, of course my own.

And last, but by no means least, to my wife, Nicola, and my son, Alex, for their patience, encouragement and occasional company during my frequent visits to the London of 375 years ago.

Introduction

When Thomas Hobbes wrote 'But for the city the Parliament never could have made the war, nor the Rump ever have murdered the King',[1] he was expressing an opinion commonly held by contemporaries that London had been critical to the outcome of the English Civil Wars. As the country's capital, and its largest city and seaport, it was the political and economic centre, and as such, its resources – manpower, money, manufacturing and armaments – could not be equalled. Despite its importance, Civil War London is a subject that, until recently, has received relatively little attention from historians outside of what is included in most histories of the war and general histories of 17th century London. And those studies which do focus on London tend to do so from a religious, political, economic or social perspective, thus overlooking just how important London was militarily.

There was scarcely an event during the English Civil Wars where London did not feature. It was the seat of government, the economic powerhouse, a major arms producer and, in the Tower of London, the country's principal arsenal. London's militia, the Trained Bands, formed the core of several of Parliament's armies during the early years of the war, but whilst the Trained Bands were in the field, London's citizens played a direct role in the defence of the capital through the construction of an 18 km circuit of earthwork fortifications, the famous 'Lines of Communication'. This wasn't the London of Samuel Pepys's diary, but it was a London that Pepys knew very well: he grew up in the City and witnessed several of its key events. Indeed, it is even possible that Pepys may even have laboured, as thousands of Londoners did, on London's fortifications. The capital was a place of execution (public executions took place in at least nine different locations in central London); it received the war's wounded and captured, and was the place of burial for many of the wars' chief protagonists.

London was certainly not a Royalist city, although the King had plenty of supporters within the capital (although the extent of a perceived Royalist 'fifth-column' is a matter for debate), but on the other hand, it was never 100 percent behind the Parliamentarian war effort either. There was a significant neutral element and those who wanted nothing more than an end to the fighting. Every party and faction that manifested itself during the period had

---

1   Thomas Hobbes, 'Behemoth or the Long Parliament' in Stephen Porter (editor), *London and the Civil War* (Basingstoke: Macmillan Press Limited, 1996), p. 1.

INTRODUCTION

its supporters in the capital, be they Parliamentarian, Royalist, Cromwellian or Republican. Radicalism was present in several parishes across London and there were a number of churches, and inns, taverns, and alehouses where radicals congregated. For Londoners in the middle of the 17th century, religion was not a detached aspect of life. It shaped political attitudes and social and economic life, and so it was also divided religiously: Episcopalian Anglicans, Catholics, Presbyterians, Independents, and a myriad of sects including Quakers and Fifth Monarchists. The ferment and ideological upheaval experienced by Londoners during the period has been compared with that experienced in Paris after 1789 and in Tehran after 1979.[2]

When King Charles I was forced to flee his capital in January 1642, he placed his cause at an enormous disadvantage. For Parliament, once it had gained control of the capital, the cornerstone of its strategy during the first 18 months or so of the Civil War was its defence. Parliament's war effort was driven from London, and whilst London did not witness much actual fighting, although three battles (Brentford in 1642 and Bow Bridge and Surbiton in 1648) did take place in what we now know as Greater London. It was from London that Parliament's army to relieve Gloucester was dispatched, and in 1649, it was to the capital that Cromwell returned from Ireland in triumph. And at Turnham Green in November 1642, a standoff between the Parliamentarian and Royalist armies could easily have become one of the largest battles of the entire conflict.

Ultimately, the real force in the capital turned out to be the army, and change came about with the military coups of 1642, 1647, 1648–49, and 1660. So whilst the City didn't witness any fighting as such (although there was plenty of civic unrest), the military was never far away from its streets, be they Royalist swordsmen, the Trained Bands, the New Model Army or General Monck's army from Scotland.

King Charles I, who reigned over the three individual Kingdoms of England, Ireland and Scotland from 1625 until 1649. (Thomas Fisher Rare Book Library, University of Toronto)

---

2   Mark Urban, *Generals: Ten British Commanders Who Shaped the World* (London: Faber and Faber Limited, 2006) p. 10.

1
London in the 1640s

Seventeenth century London was, by modern standards, small; stretching for just two miles from north to south and fewer than five from east to west, and so could be crossed on foot in less than two hours. But by 1640s standards, London was vast: only Constantinople and Paris were larger. Within its environs lived aristocracy, merchants, artisans, apprentices, and the poor, in accommodation ranging from palaces to wooden shacks. London witnessed a phenomenal growth in its population: chiefly due to a huge influx of migrants both from other areas of the country and from overseas, the population increased from 185,000 in 1600 to 355,000 in 1640 (a figure which includes some 20,000 apprentices), and an estimated 400,000 by 1650, and of these, 220,000 lived in the suburbs.[1]

The growth of London's population was even more remarkable considering the high rate of mortality, various endemic diseases and outbreaks of bubonic plague. London was no stranger to plague, and ever since the onset of the Black Death in the 1340s, it had suffered periodic epidemics. By the 17th Century, prevention had become the preferred method of controlling the disease and as epidemics in London commonly followed those in Amsterdam the enforced quarantining of incoming vessels (at Canvey Island in Essex, where ships and crews were held for 40 days) protected London, but not entirely, however. There were epidemics in 1603, 1625 and 1636. The 1625 outbreak killed some 35,000 people and caused the coronation of Charles I to be postponed until the following year, whilst the 1636 outbreak was compounded with an outbreak of typhus. Between 1638 and 1643 London was struck by a new strain of fever, due to a combination of congested conditions amongst the poor (who were the worst affected) and as a result of the deprivations of the Civil Wars.

The growth of London's population was due largely to migration; these migrants embodying the whole social spectrum, from the poor to the wealthy. To accommodate this growth, London expanded and by 1642, 'this very long city', to quote the Venetian ambassador in 1660, had grown

---

1   A. L. Beier and R. Finlay (editors), *London 1500–1700, The Making of the Metropolis* (Harlow: Longman Group Limited, 1986), p. 45.

far outside the confines of the walled Square Mile. North of the Thames it stretched from Stepney in the east to Westminster in the west, and south of the river it encompassed Lambeth, Southwark and Rotherhithe. But to 17th century Londoners, places such as High Barnet, Romford, Barking, Bromley, Croydon, Kingston, Brentford and Uxbridge were distant towns, set in the heart of the countryside. Closer to the capital, Southwark, although part of Surrey, and often much to the resentment of the inhabitants, was under varying degrees of control of the City. London's growth was over-stretching the machinery of government, and, indeed, the local forces of law and order. More affluent parts of London were to the west and during the years preceding the war there were a number of developments to cater for the more wealthy migrants to the capital. There were new developments along the Strand, around the Inns of Court, and Covent Garden, the first of London's squares. But, places like Covent Garden aside, generally speaking, the capital was 'a topographical hotchpotch with back alleys that seem to fork endlessly; sooty churches and cathedrals crawling with tatty stalls … London is a seething, chaotic, vital mess'.[2]

The most important district remained the City of London itself. With a population of around 135,000, the City was the most vital commercial centre in the country. Made up of 133 parishes and approximately 107 recognised churches, within its boundaries were the nation's chief port, handling both coastal and overseas trade, and also inland where water was favoured over unreliable roads: the River Thames enabling trade with places like Oxford; the Royal Exchange which was the Nation's chief business place for merchants; the Tower of London, the country's main arsenal; and the country's main cloth market at Blackwell Hall. The Guildhall was the seat of the government of the City and within the City's walls were more than a hundred halls of its guilds, the power bases of London's mercantile elite, but the City of London's structure of government was hierarchical rather than democratic. Not only did the guilds exercise significant influence, they resourced the Parliamentarian war effort, through the provision of arms and, most importantly, financially, as the City was regularly called upon to fund the armies of Parliament and those of Parliament's Scottish allies as well. However, the opening up of the new trade routes overseas began to challenge the established patterns of commerce, as these brought new traders who tended to be less conservative and more radical than the establishment.

In the years preceding the outbreak of Civil War the capital enjoyed a level of education that would not be seen again until the 20th century – there were a significant number of grammar and private schools in existence at the time. The absence of censorship resulted in writers combining with printers and booksellers to produce a flood of pamphlets and newssheets, reporting news from both home and abroad, and amongst them were some of the most radical literature ever published in this country. In the capital's taverns where gentry, shopkeepers and artisans freely mingled, politics was openly debated. It was this climate that led to the rise of popular political activity. Although

---

2   Matthew Green, *London: A travel guide through time* (London: Michael Joseph, 2015), pp. 183–4.

occasionally manipulated by Parliamentary leaders this activity, usually in the form of petitions and street protests, was not always partisan. However frightening this mass political activity was to some, London was not being overtaken by 'mob rule'. There was a definite sense of containment, of political direction and discipline. Attacks on private property were fairly rare and the session records show a distinct lack of prosecutions for riot. The London apprentices in all probability represent the more turbulent element of the various demonstrations and some contemporaries are careful to distinguish between 'the citizens and apprentices'. The actual composition of the crowds differs depending on the observer; the less sympathetic the eyewitness the lower the social origins of the crowd. It can be assumed that the crowds were representative of both the middle and lower orders although there were no 'aldermen, merchants or Common Councilmen' among them.[3]

There was already an east west spilt with the poorest living in the developing eastern suburbs, in marked contrast to the affluent west. Initiated by the overflow from London's growing population, the growth of the suburbs was driven by industry and commerce. Initially this was the expansion of existing trades beyond the City walls and outside the control of the Guilds, and was followed by the new industries that grew on the back of the developing overseas trade. The population of what is now known as Tower Hamlets grew faster than in any other part of the capital, and at its heart was Stepney, bordered by the City to the west, the River Lea to the east, Hackney to the north and the Thames to the south. Although largely rural, by the middle of the 17th century it had been developed along the main roads and along the river, and here it was the growth of the great merchant companies which resulted in the riverside becoming busy with docks and wharves. Limehouse, Ratcliffe and finally Wapping itself become absorbed into one, and riverside land became so valuable that mudflats and marshes were reclaimed. In the coming war, the military potential of the docks at Ratcliffe and Shadwell was not ignored, and along with Deptford, they became the cradle of the Navy. Not surprisingly, the area also would provide Parliament's navy with a number of its captains. By 1642, Tower Hamlets was already known for its radicalism, but since the Puritanism of Tower Hamlets was more radical than the conservative Puritanism of the City itself and there was the underlying danger that longstanding differences between suburbs and City would manifest themselves as rifts in London's support for Parliament.

South of the river, Southwark had long had the reputation of being the City's disreputable underbelly. Outside the City's jurisdiction, with its cockpits, theatres, brothels, bawdy taverns and alehouses, Southwark's reputation was as a place of raffish recreation, although by the outbreak of the Civil War it was starting to decline as a place of popular entertainment. Southwark also had more prisons and places of detention per square acre than anywhere else in London, and the area had a reputation for radicalism. Outside the City walls to the north lay Moorfields and the former religious sites of Charterhouse, the Priory of St John and the Nunnery of St Mary. Further

---

3 Brian Manning, *The English People and the English Revolution* (London: Bookmarks, 1991), pp. 154–5.

LONDON IN THE 1640S

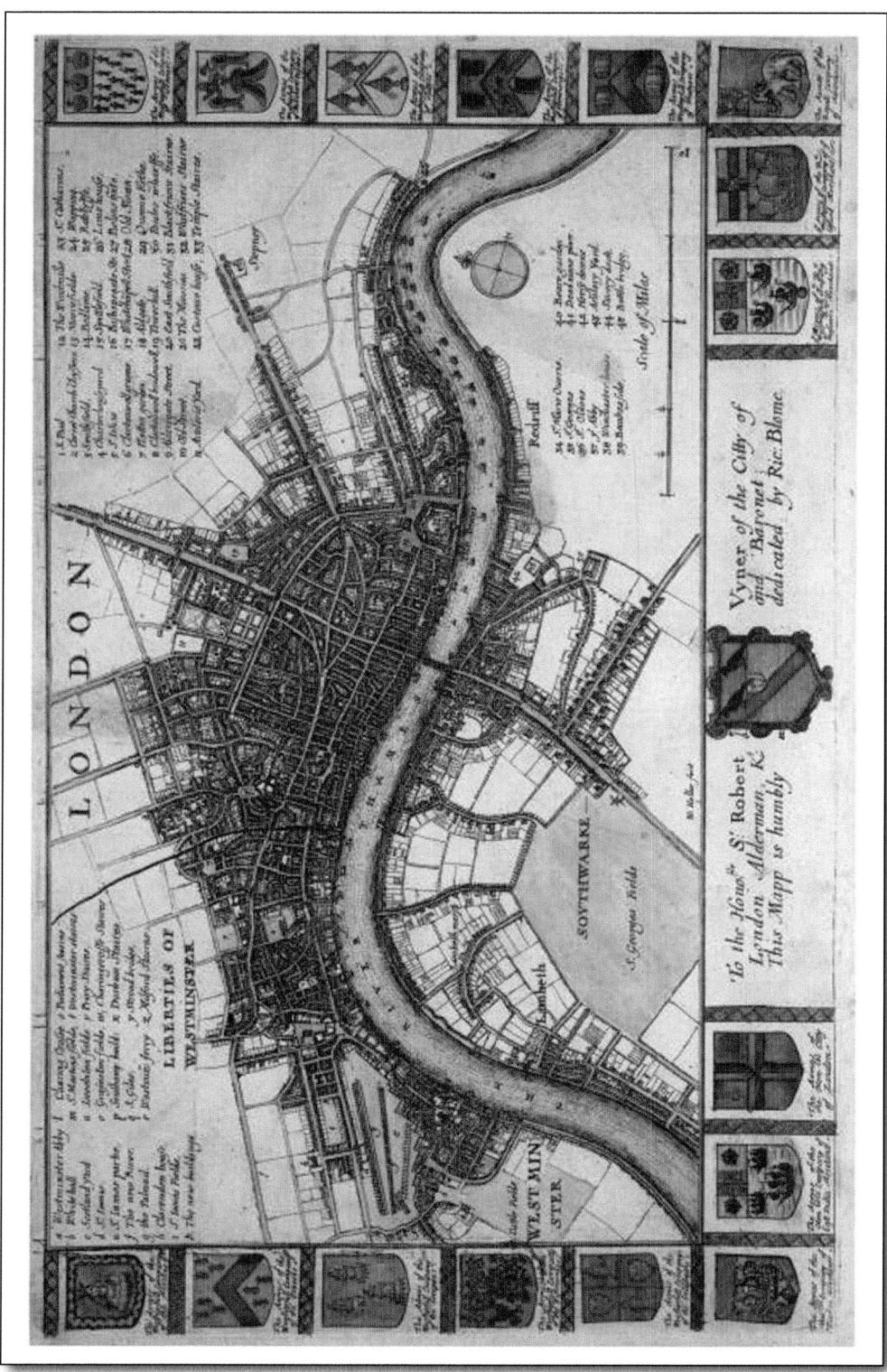

Hollar's map of London just before the Great Fire. The capital had changed relatively little during the preceding two decades. (Thomas Fisher Rare Book Library, University of Toronto)

north and east were such villages as Hackney and Islington, and the land in-between remained almost free of buildings until the 18th century. This area was well known for its country inns and pubs, whilst Clerkenwell was gaining a reputation for its less salubrious venues, including theatres, inns and brothels. Another feature of this area was the Water House at the head of the New River, an artificial river which flowed from springs in Amwell and Chadwell in Hertfordshire. Carefully surveyed, it followed a meandering route until it reached Islington where a system of sluices in the Water House itself took the water into two great basins. From here, the water flowed via a system of cisterns and through great pipes of hollowed elm trunks into the City. London households subscribed to this water supply and in 1643 some of the profits of this scheme funded the Parliamentarian war-effort in Shropshire.[4]

The growth of London during the 17th century can be gauged by the expansion of the Bills of Mortality, the weekly list of numbers of deaths and their cause, and during the first half of the century the area covered by the Bills was regularly enlarged to encompass neighbouring parishes to the east and the north. London's Civil War defences, the Lines of Communication, defined the boundary of the capital between 1643 and 1647 and continued to do so after the defences were demolished – for administrative purposes, the term 'within the Lines of Communication' was a commonly used definition for the capital.

By 1642, the City's walls had long ceased to confine the expanding population, and now formed a boundary between the City itself, and the suburbs. But the wall still existed: medieval in origin (although parts dated back to Roman times), comprising of 3.4 km (just over 2 miles) of wall, fronted by the City ditch and breached by eight gates. Although continually improved throughout the medieval period, they had not received any major attention since 1477. This is not to say that they were totally neglected, however: there is evidence of repair work during the Tudor period (for example near Wood Street). Writing towards the end of Elizabeth's reign, John Stow described the rebuilding of four of the City gates between 1472 and 1586. All the gates had lost their barbicans and one, the Tower of London Postern, was in a ruinous state. Stow also mentions two breaches in the walls, the first near to St Bartholomew's Hospital and the second between Fleet Bridge and the Thames. Turning to the City ditch, Stow found it 'neglected and forced either to a very narrow and the same a filthy channel, or altogether stopped up for gardens planted, and houses built thereon, even to the very wall, and in many places upon both ditch and wall houses be built'.[5] By 1552, the western part of the ditch had been filled in for health reasons as the rubbish dumped in the ditch had become a hazard to the newly founded Christ's Hospital Orphanage. Therefore, although the walled defences existed, they would require some remedial work before they could be defendable and, more importantly, they would only be able to protect a small area of the capital and its inhabitants, although these were London's elite.

---

4   Jonathan Worton, *To Settle the Crown* (Solihull: Helion and Company, 2016), p. 147.
5   John Stow, *A Survey of London* (Stroud: The History Press, 2005), p. 50.

2

The Winter Crisis, 1641–42

Charles I had ruled without Parliament since 1629. But his 'Personal Rule' (or 'Eleven Years' Tyranny', dependant upon your point of view) might had lasted longer and it not been for events in Scotland. Charles' Archbishop of Canterbury, William Laud, attempted to restore discipline and order to the Church of England according to the rules laid down in the earliest days of the English Reformation. But this was contrary to Puritan opinion, and his doctrines were regarded as dangerously close to Roman Catholicism. To make matters worse, attempts to force uniformity on the Church of Scotland met with disaster, resulting in the Bishops' Wars of 1639–40 (the cost of raising a 40,000 strong English army to fight the Scots was £900,000, nearly double the Crown's annual revenues).[1] The financial might of the City was vital and whilst the King might be able to rule without Parliament, he still needed the financial support of the City, which provided financial assistance in the form of loans to the King during the First Bishop's War. But ultimately this was not enough, and in 1640 Charles was forced to recall Parliament. Under the leadership of John Pym, Parliament made a number of demands from the King in return for their financial support, demands ultimately including the sacrifice of his most able advisor, Thomas Wentworth, Earl of Strafford. If this was not enough, the Scots had inflicted an embarrassing defeat on the King.

When rebellion broke out in Ireland in the autumn 1641, the City again initially funded the armed response by granting a substantial loan. But it was the raising of an army for Ireland which was yet another contentious issue, with Pym concerned that the King might use the troops not against the rebellious Irish but against his opponents in England. Thus control of the military, be it a local militia, or a full army, was a major issue for both sides. Towards the end of 1641, Charles visited Scotland in an attempt to heal the scars of the Bishops Wars. By the time he returned to London from Edinburgh in November 1641, he had regained much of the support he had lost, whilst in Parliament, support for John Pym had lessened, and by

---

1   M. C. Fissel, *The Bishops' Wars, Charles I's Campaigns against Scotland, 1638–40* (Cambridge: Cambridge University Press, 1994), p. 111.

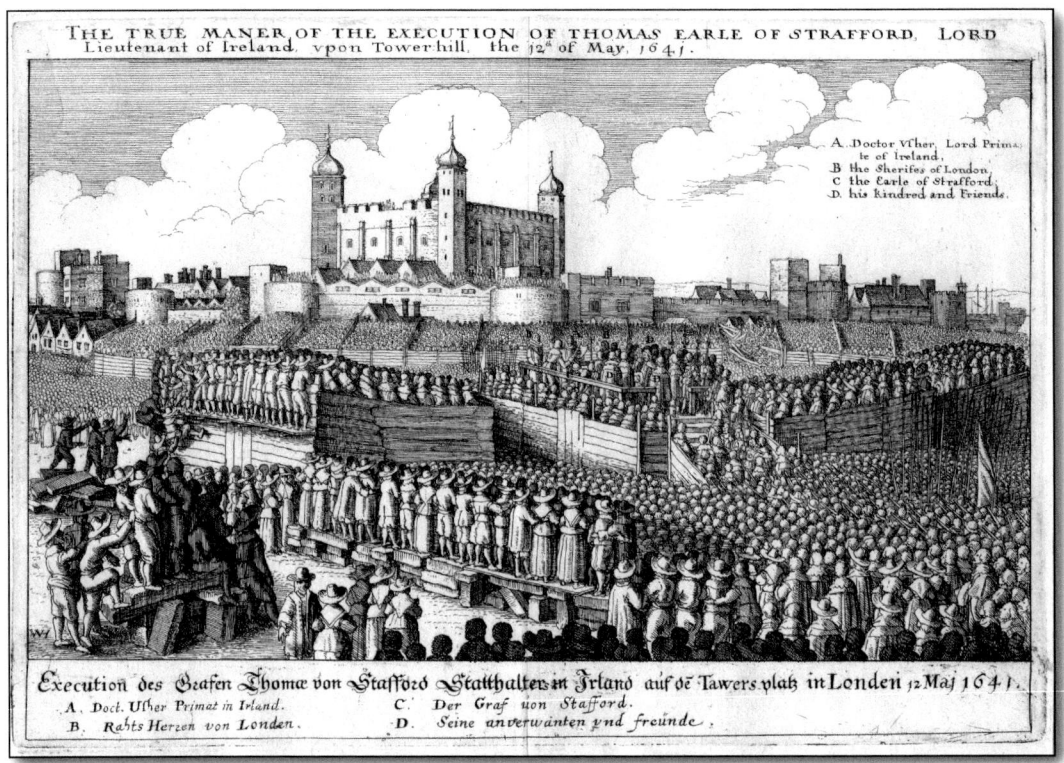

Hollar's representation of the execution of the Earl of Strafford on Tower Hill on 12 May 1641. Hastily produced, it proved to be a very popular work with Londoners who disliked King Charles's most able advisor. (Thomas Fisher Rare Book Library, University of Toronto)

December 1641 there was a sizeable Royalist minority in Parliament – not only those who were actual Royalists, but also those who felt that the previous reforms demanded by Pym had gone far enough and were opposed to any extremism. Thus the Grand Remonstrance, a document put together by Pym and his allies listing all the grievances perpetrated by the King, was passed by a narrow margin of 159 votes to 148.

But whilst the King may have won over the City's leadership, distrust amongst ordinary Londoners remained, and it was events in the City of London which fundamentally altered the political landscape, as the elections to the City's Court of Common Council in December 1641 resulted in a comfortable majority for Pym's supporters. And whilst the King was appealing to the City of London to take steps to prevent the unrest at Westminster, these 'new men' were instrumental in creating the Committee of Safety which took control of the City's militia away from the Lord Mayor. This was just the start, as over the coming weeks supporters of the King within the City's government were forced to resign, or retired, or, in the case of Lord Mayor Sir Richard Gurney, were ultimately arrested and sent to the Tower. With tensions rising, it was up to the Trained Bands to maintain order, even though many of them were the masters of the apprentices and were in sympathy with the demonstrators. During December 1641 there was a riot in Newgate, and Londoners prevented the Bishops taking their places in the House of Lords.

The end of the Bishops' Wars also brought about the problem of many demobbed soldiers who descended on London looking for their pay and employment. Some joined the Royalist Colonel Thomas Lunsford who

THE WINTER CRISIS, 1641–42

Hollar's view of the Palace of Whitehall, dominated by Inigo Jones's Banqueting House. (Thomas Fisher Rare Book Library, University of Toronto)

had recently been appointed Lieutenant of the Tower of London, and these 'Swordsmen' quickly clashed with the apprentices and others who demonstrated against the King. There was a public demonstration against the Royal appointment of Lunsford as Lieutenant of the Tower, an appointment which appeared to confirm suspicions that the King intended to use force against opposition, and when petitioners clashed with Lunsford and his 'Swordsmen' at Westminster, further disturbances followed. By the end of December it was reported that 'the citizens for the most part shut up their shops, and all gentlemen provide themselves with arms'.[2] As one observer wrote, 'the war was begun in our street before the King or the Parliament had any armies'.

The turning point of the entire crisis occurred on 4 January 1642 when the King entered the Commons to arrest five members of Parliament: John Pym, John Hampden, Denzil Holles, Sir Arthur Hesilrige and William Strode. When asked by the King where the five were, William Lenthall, the Speaker of the House, famously replied, 'I have neither eyes to see nor tongue to speak in this place but as this House is pleased to direct me'. The five had been forewarned and took refuge in the City, followed by the rest of the House, which adjourned itself to the Guildhall. The Parliamentary leadership had, in effect, thrown themselves upon the loyalty of the citizens of London. Despite the efforts of the King, who came into the City the following day to demand it hand over the five members, it was the cry of 'The Privileges of Parliament' which echoed in his ears'.[3] The hostile demonstrations of the citizens made an impression on the King, who 'had the worst day in London ... that ever he had'. Fearful that he and his family could no longer feel safe from the mob, on 10 January he fled from Whitehall, first to Hampton Court

---

2 W. D. Hamilton (editor), *Calender of State Papers, Domestic Series, 1641–43* (London: HMSO, 1887), Vol. 1, p. 214.
3 *The English Civil War – A Contemporary Account* (London: Caliban Books, 1996), Vol. 2, p. 163..

and then on to Windsor. By doing so, he had abandoned the wealth and resources of the capital to his enemies. In the end, the country was brought to the brink of civil war by religious and political issues, complicated by the ambitions of three different nations existing under a single crown. Yet what tipped the country over the edge were aggressively opposed personalities, each becoming more and more entrenched and unable to suffer the loss of face that backing down would entail.

As the country drifted towards Civil War during the spring of 1642 there were few who doubted that the King would attempt to win back his capital, by force if necessary. London had its Trained Bands, but these aside, London was largely undefended. Although the City walls existed, they would require attention before they could be used and then they would only be able to protect the wealthier City, leaving the suburbs undefended. However, in 1642, the walls were the only defences that existed. Orders were given for the gates and portcullises to be seen to, and the chains and posts, the only existing barriers to those routes into the capital not protected by the walls, to be repaired. But despite this, in the summer of 1642, so much depended upon London's Trained Bands.

3

The Trained Bands

Formed during the reign of Henry VIII, the City of London's militia, the London Trained Bands, were considered the elite of Tudor England's 'General Levey' by the reign of Elizabeth I, and represented the standard by which the county militias looked to aspire. Their discipline and efficiency was due to a great extent to the relationship and affiliation with the Honourable Artillery Company, and by the time of the 1585 Royal review at Greenwich, their front line was said to be 4,000 in number, all musketeers. During the reign of James I, the Trained Bands were reorganised first into companies and then into four regiments, North, South, East and West, under the command of the Lord Mayor, thus the office of Lord Mayor had significant military might. In peacetime the militia, officered by the gentry, was, in the words of Christopher Hill, 'the army of property'.

In January 1642, a joint committee of the House of Commons and the City's Committee of Safety appointed Philip Skippon, a veteran of the Thirty Years' War, to command the Trained Bands with the rank of Sergeant-Major-General. Thus, by the spring of 1642, the King's opponents had not only gained control of London but also of the Trained Bands, which, although only 6,000 strong at the time of the winter crisis, would form the basis of Parliament's army in the event of war. Following his appointment, Skippon set about reforming the four regiments; from these he created six new ones with colonels and captains appointed from the old formations, and vacancies were filled through the promotion of subalterns or the granting of commissions to recent graduates of the Honourable Artillery Company, although there was still a dominance of aldermen amongst senior officers (colonels of five out of the six City regiments were aldermen, including Isaac Penington who was Colonel of the White regiment). Recruitment to the rank and file was also extended and included all able-bodied men within the City. The six new regiments, each around 1,200 men strong, were identified by a colour (Red, White, Yellow, Blew, Greene, and Orange) and were ranked in accordance of the status of their colonels.

The first in order of precedence was the Red Regiment, which was recruited from the wards of Aldgate, Tower and Billingsgate. The White Regiment, recruited from the wards of Cornhill, Langbourne, Lime Street, Broad Street and Bishopsgate, was ranked next. Third was the Yellow Regiment, which

Phillip Skippon, appointed commander of the London Trained Bands in 1642, and Captain-General of the Honourable Artillery Company between 1657 and 1660. Skippon commanded the New Model Army's infantry at Naseby in June 1645. (The Turton Collection)

was recruited from the wards of Farringdon Within, Castle Baynard and Aldersgate. Next was the Blew Regiment, which was recruited from the wards of Bridge, Walbrook, Bread Street, Candlewick, Dowgate, Vintry, Cheap and Queenhithe. The wards of Coleman Street, Bassishaw and Cripplegate were the recruiting area for the Greene Regiment. Finally was the Orange Regiment, and uniquely, this was the only regiment recruited from outside the City wall (as well as from the ward of Farringdon Without).[1] The Trained Bands were placed in readiness, although here Parliament faced a dilemma: whilst they would be an effective core for Parliament's field army, they were equally needed to defend the capital and would have to remain close to London to do so. In any case, how willing would the Trained Bands be to leave their families, homes and businesses unprotected? So they were neither available to join the main Parliamentary army under the command of Robert Devereux, 3rd Earl of Essex, or to guard the distant approaches to London. To address this, on 1 September 1642 the Court of Common Council ordered the raising of two new separate regiments of foot. But in November 1642, it was the Trained Bands that marched out from the City with Essex's army to confront the royalists at Turnham Green.

By early 1643, the Trained Bands of Westminster, Southwark and Tower Hamlets had also been placed under Skippon's command. Early in the same year, the Trained Bands were augmented by the creation of a regiment of dragoons, and six auxiliary regiments of foot (known as the Red, White, Yellow, Blew, Greene, and Orange auxiliaries), the latter intended to main London's fortifications, thus freeing the regular Trained Bands for service elsewhere. Finally, auxiliary regiments from Westminster, Southwark and Tower Hamlets were also formed, bringing the total strength of London's Trained Bands to 18 regiments, a strength on paper of some 18,000 soldiers. But the strength of each regiment varied considerably: at a muster on 26 September 1643 it was recorded that the Greene regiment's strength was 503 musketeers and 297 pikemen (a musket to pike ratio approximately 5:3 – the typical ratio and that followed by the New Model Army was 2:1), whilst the Westminster Trained Bands mustered 1,084 musketeers and 854 pikemen.

---

1 See Keith Roberts, *London and Liberty* (Leigh-on-Sea: Partizan Press, 1987). Chapter IV details the Trained Bands of the City of London, whilst those of the suburbs are covered in chapter VI.

London's militia also included two regiments of horse, both of which fought at Newport Pagnell in 1643.

However, despite the City's concerns about the loss of so much of its workforce to military service, such was Parliament's need for troops that the auxiliaries also found themselves serving outside London and at the end of September 1644 a proposition was considered for 'the raising and maintaining a Regiment of 1,200 foote souldiers to be constantly imployed in keeping the Forts, and Works about the City and within the Line of Communication'. There is, however, no record of such a unit having been actually formed. Whilst again not part of the Trained Bands, in November 1643, Parliament commissioned Londoner Thomas Taylor to raise a company of Archers. This was two months after reports had reached London from Oxford that 'the King hath two regiments of Bows and Arrowes'.[2]

Although the Trained Bands were created to defend London, during the First Civil War they saw action in most of Parliament's campaigns in the south. In 1643, they participated in the relief of Gloucester and the subsequent first battle of Newbury (20 September 1643).[3] Later the same year, they marched to secure Newport Pagnell, besieged Basing House and fought at the battle of Alton and the storming of Grafton House. On 20 December 1643, the Trained Bands returned to London, a cause for celebration in itself, bringing back with them a large number of Royalist prisoners who were dispersed to several prisons including Newgate, Bridewell and Ely House. In 1644, Trained Band regiments saw victory at the battle of Cheriton (29 March 1644), but were less successful at Cropredy Bridge (29 June 1644) where, in their first campaign, the Tower Hamlets Trained Bands (who normally provided the garrison for the Tower), deserted en masse and returned home. The Trained Bands also took part in Essex's disastrous western campaign which ended in defeat at Lostwithiel (31 August–1 September 1644), and they also fought at the second battle of Newbury (27 October 1644). Trained Bands units also formed part of the garrisons of Weymouth, Reading, Abingdon and Reading.

Whilst the Trained Bands were at their most effective when London was directly threatened, there were other times when they did excel themselves (the relief of Gloucester for example). But for much of the time, they showed

Robert Devereux, Earl of Essex, the 'Lord General of the Forces Raised by the Parliament of England', and the victor of Turnham Green. (Thomas Fisher Rare Book Library, University of Toronto)

---

2   *Mercurius Civicus* (Reading: Tyger's Head Books, 2013–14), Vol. 1, p. 144.
3   British Library, Thomason Tracts, E669.f.7-(33) *An order by the Committee for the Militia for the relief of Gloucester.*

a marked reluctance to be away from the capital for any length of time and would not suffer the hardships of campaign without complaint. Many would desert (according to the Venetian Ambassador, Gerolamo Agostini, many served reluctantly, under threat of severe punishment), forcing their luckless commander to send the rest home. Away from London, the Trained Bands operated better under the Earl of Essex than they did under Sir William Waller. The type of warfare waged by Essex was rather textbook and was that taught by officers at the Artillery Garden. Waller waged a different type of warfare – campaigns in bad weather, assaults on fortified positions, fighting in wooded or broken ground – and this did not suit the Trained Bands at all.[4]

After the Newbury campaign in 1644 the Trained Bands were not again involved on the battlefield. This was due largely to the creation of the New Model Army, as well as the reluctance of the City authorities and the soldiers themselves for the Trained Bands to participate in operations outside the immediate vicinity of the capital. But even so, it is unlikely that all 18 regiments were not back in London again until early 1646, and certainly by 19 May they mustered together again. Thus in theory, London had an army of some 18,000 to face the New Model Army, now suffering desertions of its own by Londoners within its ranks, when it advanced on London in the summer in 1647. Yet when called upon to muster, only the Westminster Trained Bands were present in any strength, the rest viewing this as an advance on Parliament rather than on London and Londoners. Even so, once the New Model had gained control of London, the officers of the Trained Bands were purged, London's defences dismantled and responsibility for the garrisoning of both the Tower and Westminster was taken away from London's militia; although during the crisis of spring 1648, the Trained Bands returned to both, freeing the New Model to focus on dealing with Royalist insurgency.

---

4   Keith Roberts, 'Citizen Soldiers: The Military Power of the City of London', in Stephen Porter (editor), *London and the Civil War* (Basingstoke: Macmillan Press Limited, 1996), pp. 106–7.

4

A City at War, 1642–46

The Trained Bands did not exhaust the manpower available from London as larger numbers of Londoners were also recruited into Parliament's field armies. But after the initial rush of recruits, the citizens of the City were reluctant to join Parliament's armies, which forced recruiters to look towards the suburbs for recruits. There is evidence that some were impressed, although the Royalist newsbook *Mercurius Aulicus* of 26 August 1643 probably exaggerated its claim that poor men were press-ganged into Parliament's armies. Others would have gone to war for adventure or because of peer pressure, for instance, Anthony Fletcher cites how Stepney apprentices and journeymen enlisted following a sermon at the end of July 1642. Undoubtedly, some would have gone to war for profit – histories of the Trained Bands make several references to the looting and the pillaging of the soldiers. But for the majority, the protection of their families, homes and livelihoods were uppermost in their minds. A number did take this notion of self-preservation to extremes, only with reluctance would they serve and would desert when things became too dangerous or uncomfortable. The enthusiasm of Londoners to serve in Parliament's armies at the outbreak of the war (according to one account, enlistments at the New Artillery Garden on 26 July 1642 numbered 5,000 citizens, and 3,000 apprentices two days later[1]) had waned by the end of 1644, with the capital providing hardly any volunteers at all.

The First Civil War commenced during the summer of 1642, and its opening campaign took place in the Midlands. The first major battle, Edgehill on 23 October, was inconclusive but it did leave the way clear for the King to advance on London. Recent reassessment of the Edgehill campaign suggests that the Parliamentarian strategy was not for Essex's army to block the King's advance on London, but instead force it before London's defences where it would be defeated by Parliamentarian forces. The defence of London in the autumn of 1642 was not panicked, but it was certainly hasty. The Tower of London was stripped of much of its artillery to arm Essex's army, but the

---

1 BL, Thomason Tracts, E202-(28) *A Perfect Diurnal of Passages in Parliament*, 25 July–1 August 1642.

CIVIL WAR LONDON

Robert Rich, Earl of Warwick. Parliamentarian admiral, he was appointed to command of Parliament's new army in October 1642. (Thomas Fisher Rare Book Library, University of Toronto)

threat of a Royalist advance on London was such that batteries and less sophisticated forms of defence were thrown up around London. The batteries had to be armed, but fortunately, the guns removed from the Tower were replaced by imports from France and the Netherlands and by weapons seized from the homes of Royalists. But this could not address the shortage of gunners, a problem which continued well beyond the autumn of 1642.

The Trained Bands themselves were placed in preparedness, although here Parliament faced a dilemma: whilst they would be an effective core for Parliament's field army, they were equally needed to defend the capital and would have to remain close to London to do so. So they were nether available to join Essex or to guard the distant approaches to London. To address this, on 1 September 1642, the Court of Common Council ordered the raising of two new regiments of foot, under the commands of Alderman John Venn and Alderman Randall Mainwaring. By the end of October 1642, Venn's regiment was garrisoning Windsor Castle. But this was not enough, and on 21 October, instructions were sent to the Lord Lieutenants of 15 counties in East Anglia and south-east England to raise troops from their militias and volunteers. The Earl of Warwick the Parliamentarian admiral, was given command of this new army,[2] but given the Royalist threat, only those areas close enough to be protected by London felt secure enough to raise troops. Few officers from the Trained Bands joined Essex's army in the summer of 1642, but the formation of this second army saw a number of Trained Bands officers accept commissions in the new army, whilst several other officers were members of the Honourable Artillery Company. The resulting vacancies were filled through promotion within the Trained Bands and by granting commissions to other members of the Artillery Garden. Thus this new force, which comprised about 6,000 infantry by 12 November, weakened the same Trained Bands it intended to reinforce.

Despite the advice of his nephew, Prince Rupert, to make a rapid advance on London, the King approached his capital slowly, advancing along the Thames Valley, and overwhelming Parliamentarian forces at Brentford on 12 November before meeting 24,000 Parliamentarian troops under the Earl of Essex at Turnham Green the next day. The Battle of Turnham Green is one of the defining moments in London's Civil War. The troops Essex

---

2   *The English Civil War – A Contemporary Account*, Vol. 2, p. 318

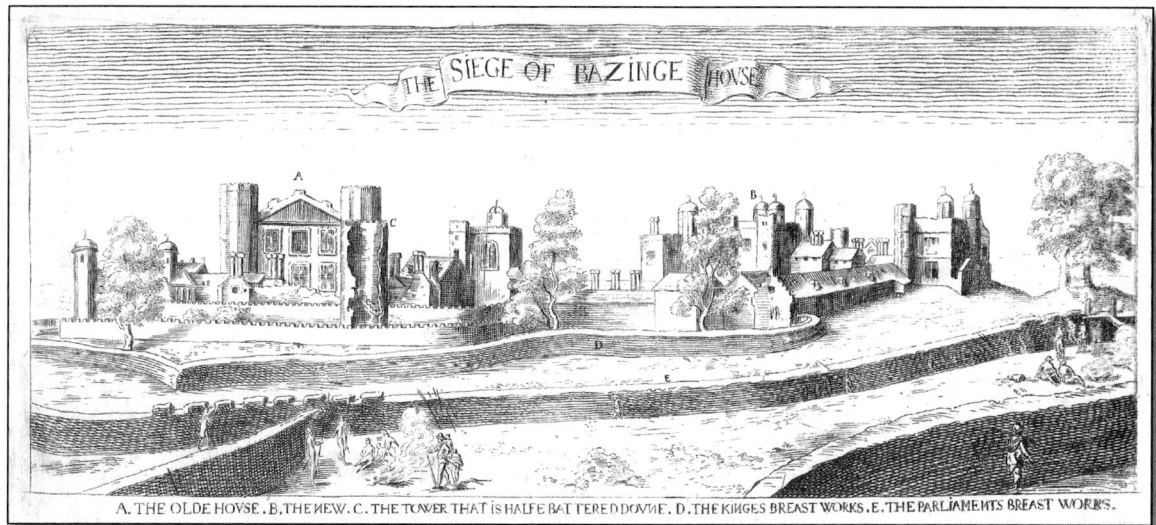

Basing House – attacked by the London Trained Bands and defended by Marmaduke Rawdon's 'London' regiment. (The Turton Collection)

commanded that day included a contingent of the Trained Bands, elements of Warwick's 'new army', plus a number of new recruits who flocked to London's defence in the face of the Royalist threat. Even Londoners not under arms provided support by providing hundreds of wagons of supplies which were subsequently sent to aid the inhabitants of Brentford. In the war of words, the Royalist attack on Brentford was an absolute boon for Parliamentarian propagandists. The King's actions had provided them with much ammunition, and they likened it to the atrocities in Germany, such as the sacking of Magdeburg, a decade earlier. The war of words was fought with as much vigour as the actual battles and sieges were, but it was a war that Parliament always had the best of, and even before the fighting had started, Pym used the printed word to successfully manage popular discontent over a range of political and religious issues.

Yet the King was not without his support. In December 1641, the King's support came from existing soldiers, gentlemen and students from the Inns of Court, and not all of these had fled London by the end of the following year. Added to which were a number of Parliamentarian supporters having second thoughts and, according to Giovannie Giustinian, the Venetian ambassador, several captains of the Trained Bands had resigned, and the King's supporters felt bold enough to wear rose-coloured ribbons in their hats. Matters came to a head in early October 1642 when Royalists resisted Puritan attempts to wreck the organ in St Paul's Cathedral.[3] Parliament acted decisively: they ordered the Lord Mayor to close the cathedral and authorised what amounted to a 'stop and search' policy on anyone suspected of having Royalist sympathies, whilst those who refused to pay taxes or loans would be considered Royalist delinquents. Close censorship was introduced and then the houses and stables of anyone suspected of supporting the King were searched and horses and arms confiscated. As a result, many Londoners were imprisoned. Then Catholics were forced to leave the capital, and suspect

---

3   *Ibid.*, p. 312.

Wenceslaus Hollar (1607–1677) – the 'man who drew London'. (Thomas Fisher Rare Book Library, University of Toronto)

clergymen were removed from their livings and those who challenged Parliament from the pulpit were arrested.

Many Royalists fled London and joined the King in Oxford. Notable amongst these was Marmaduke Rawdon, who was actually Lieutenant Colonel of the Red Regiment of the London Trained Bands until early 1643, but in March he left the capital, and on reaching Oxford, formed a regiment of foot, at his own expense, officered from his London contacts, all of whom had been members of the Honourable Artillery Company. Whilst the Trained Bands were more adept in the field, Rawdon's regiment was effective behind fortifications, a reputation gained whilst part of the garrison of Basing House. One of Rawdon's companies, and the first to reach Basing House in July 1643, was commanded by Robert Peake, who had been a London print seller in civilian life. Within the ranks pf Peake's company were, at one time or another, the painter and engraver William Faithorne, the artist William Dobson (although Dobson remained at Oxford) and the etcher Wenceslaus Hollar. Thus Peake's company could be seen as the original 'Artists Rifles'.

Encountering former brothers in arms from the London Trained Bands at the end of 1643, Rawdon's remained at Basing House until March 1645, although Peake's company was transferred to the regiment of John Paulet, 5th Marquis of Winchester, the owner of Basing. Peake himself went on to command the Honourable Artillery Company.[4] Rawdon's regiment itself formed the garrison of Faringdon House in Berkshire from May 1645,[5] from where it undertook a number of raids against Parliamentarian positions, including Andover in December 1645. In March 1646, Faringdon was besieged by the New Model Army, and Rawdon himself died of pneumonia on 28 April. He was buried at All Saint's Church, Faringdon, but shortly after the ceremony, an enemy mortar shell hit the church, killing three soldiers. The regiment was disbanded not long after the surrender of the house in June 1646. Rawdon was not the only Trained Bands officer to join the King: Rawdon's son-in-law, Colonel Edmund Foster, and Captain Richard Hacket from the Blew Regiment, both left London in 1643.

But London's greatest Royalist soldier was Sir George Lisle. Born in 1615, baptised at St Gregory by St Paul's, and raised in Westminster, his father was a well-connected publisher. Lisle fought during the Thirty Years' War, before serving as a captain during the Bishops' Wars, and then, at the outbreak of

---

4 The author is grateful to Andrew Robertshaw for sharing his research on Rawdon's regiment.
5 Originally Berkshire, but part of Oxfordshire since 1974.

the English Civil War, he was commissioned lieutenant colonel. He fought at Edgehill, Chalgrove (18 June 1643), and the first battle of Newbury where he was wounded. A popular and brave officer, Lisle went on to fight at Cheriton, Lostwithiel, and the second battle of Newbury. He was the governor of Faringdon during the winter of 1644–45, and whilst governor, successfully repulsed an attack by Oliver Cromwell. But with his skills as a field commander desperately needed by the King, he soon left Faringdon and was replaced by Rawdon. He fought at Naseby (14 June 1645) where he was again wounded. Knighted the following December, he was in Oxford when it surrendered in June 1646, after which he returned to London. He took up arms again during the Kentish rebellion in the spring of 1648, but following the defeat at Maidstone (1 June 1648), along with George Goring, 1st Earl of Norwich, Lisle led the survivors northwards, across the Thames and ultimately to Colchester where, following the town's surrender after an 11 week siege, on 27 August 1648 he was executed by firing squad outside Colchester Castle, becoming a Royalist martyr.[6]

The memorial to Sir George Lisle and Sir Charles Lucas, executed by firing squad after the surrender of Colchester on 28 August 1648. (David Flintham)

With the flight of many leading Royalists, Parliament's heavy-handed approach prevented a major Royalist insurrection. But this did not prevent small-scale pro-Royalist protests and plots, the most notable of which was the Waller Plot in May 1643. Named after the Royalist poet, Edmund Waller (though he was only a relatively minor player), the conspirators looked to secure the capital for the King. The plot was soon discovered and Waller, and his fellow conspirators, Richard Challoner, and Waller's brother-in-law Nathaniel Tomkin, were arrested. Waller confessed 'whatever he had said heard, thought or seen, and all that he knew ... or suspected of others', and was fined and banished, but Challoner and Tomkins were less fortunate, and were executed on 5 July 1643.

Whilst there was not an organised Royalist fifth column, there was plenty of suspected Royalist activity for the newsbook *Mercurius Civicus* to report: this might be Royalist prisoners escaping from prison, Royalist 'agents' dressed as women being apprehended (in New Fish Street), and the houses of suspected Royalists being raided. In May 1643, the house of Colonel Hercules Hollyland in Smithfield was raided (Hollyland himself was in Oxford with the King),[7] whilst Royalists were blamed for starting fires

---

6   See Serena Jones, *No Armour But Courage: Colonel Sir George Lisle, 1615–1648* (Solihull: Helion & Company Limited, 2016).
7   *Mercurius Civicus* (Reading: Tyger's Head Books, 2013–14), Vol. 1, p. 27.

on 6 and 8 April 1644 in the Newgate and Old Bailey area,[8] and taverns on Aldersgate Street and in Islington were identified as meeting places for 'London Malignants'. Sir Kenelm Digby was arrested at Mile End whilst observing the construction of the fortifications and on 12 August 1643, the houses of suspected Royalists in Westminster and Southwark were searched and a 'great store of Armes and Ammunitions' found.[9] There were citizens who would inform the authorities about Royalist activities, most notably the nurse Elizabeth Alkin (also known as 'Parliament Joan') who successfully uncovered underground Royalist printing presses.

But the most apparent Royalist presence during the Civil Wars were the Royalist prisoners of war who were dispersed across a number of London prisons: Newgate, Bridewell, Lambeth Palace, and a number in Southwark. In February 1644 the order went out for a number of these prisoners 'to be fetch out of those prisons and be shipt for Barmudas or some other forraigne Plantations'.[10] Ely House housed well-to-do Royalist prisoners, those who could pay for their keep. But for the rest, they were dependent on a small allowance from Parliament, and on charity.

Although Parliament had been, on the whole, successful in supressing the Royalist sympathies of Londoners, ensuring continued loyalty to the Parliamentary cause was a different matter, and it was here that London's reputation for popular protest brought it into conflict with the capital's leaders. There were times when the Royalist threat to Londoners, their families and their homes was alone sufficient to persuade them to come to London's defence. But once the immediate threat had past, what then their loyalty? Thus the fortifications were nearly as much about containing an insurrection by Londoners as they were about protecting London from attack, something noted by the Venetian Secretary in March 1643: 'The shape they [the fortifications] take betrays that they are not only for defence against the royal armies, but also against tumults of the citizens, and to ensure a prompt obedience on all occasions'.[11]

And as Peter Harrington suggests "the fact that the London defences resembled siegework lines of circumvallation rather than defences may have been more than coincidental."[12] Also, the medieval City Walls served as a barrier between the wealthy City parishes and the poorer suburbs.

Parliament's control of the press was another key element in their control over London. Propagandists were quick to spread fears of Royalist attacks, citing the sack of Magdeburg in 1631, and, more recently, events in Ireland. However, there was a balance to ensure such fears resulted in support of the Parliamentarian war effort and did not develop into widespread defeatism. George Thomason, a London bookseller, collected a copy of every publication he came across (and thus establishing a fascinating resource

---

8   *Ibid.*, Vol. 2, p. 94.
9   *Ibid.*, Vol. 1, p. 83.
10 *Ibid.*, Vol .2, p. 58.
11 *The English Civil War – A Contemporary Account*, Vol. 3, p. 33.
12 Peter Harrington, *English Civil War Fortifications 1642-5* (Oxford: Osprey Publishing, 2003), p. 43.

for future historians). In 1640 in collected 24 titles, 721 in 1641, 2,134 in 1642 and between 1643 and 1647, an average of 1,413 titles a year (despite Parliamentary attempts at regulation), and a further 2,036 in 1648.

The fact that the capital escaped any major fighting (Brentford excepted) did not mean that Londoners escaped destruction to their property. On 28 October 1642 for instance, the House of Commons ordered the demolition of property outside the City walls, to deny any attacking force cover and to present the defenders with a clear field of fire. However, a similar order concerning property immediately inside the walls was never made (the space that would have been created would have been packed with earth to reinforce the walls). This was not so much due to tactical nativity but because of the potential hostile reaction by owners.

London paid a heavy price for the great circuit of earthworks that were thrown up to protect the capital. Great tracts of land had to be given up, not only that which was covered by the defences themselves. In order to prevent erosion and to provide some additional strength the defences were faced in turf, which was stripped from great areas of pasture, land that could not be grazed upon for several years after. Local land was flooded and the Royalist newsheet, *Mercurius Aulicus*, states that the fortifications involved 'digging very deep Trenches and Ditches to be filled with water from the New River and the river of Lee which runs by Bow'. In addition to the damage to land, the defences required many buildings to be demolished. In 1643 for instance, Parliament issued an order 'that all and every the sheds, on the Outside of the Walls of the said City, adjoining to the same be speedily pulled down and demolished', and subsequently houses were removed in Whitechapel.

It was not just enlistment that caused a scarcity of labour. The threat of Royalist attack caused many to flee the capital, and in March 1643 the Venetian ambassador reported that 'already a large number of houses are empty, some of the shops closed and the rest contain little or no merchandise'.[13] Labour shortages and the damage to land and property caused by the defences were not the only hardship as Royalist control of north-eastern England during the first two years of the war prevented the supply of coal to London. The resulting fuel crisis was probably the most acute hardship suffered by Londoners, especially during the cold and wet winter of 1642–43. Even as late as April 1644, the Venetian Ambassador felt that 'His Majesty … hopes to reduce London to submission by fear and hardship'.[14] This hardship continued even after Newcastle had fallen to the Scots army who then possessed 'a great advantage over London'.

The scarcity of coal resulted in the switch to wood as the main domestic fuel with the result that the price of wood increased, and 'Parliament … decided to have trees cut down for 60 miles around [London]'. The shortage of coal disrupted industry and even the manufacture of firearms was interrupted. By 1644 the fuel situation had deteriorated so much that Parliament was forced to issue 'An Ordinance for the provision of Turff and

---

13 *The English Civil War – A Contemporary Account*, Vol. 3, p. 29.
14 Ibid., p. 33.

Peate for the Cities of London and Westminster and the Surburbs thereof'. As an acknowledgement to the hardships suffered by the poor, this ordinance made particular provision to ensure they would be first served.

The financial burden on London and Londoners was immense: there were duties on many foodstuffs, and during 1643 and 1644, hardly a month went by without a new ordinance requiring London to fund new troops, an existing army or the fortifications for instance. There were less formal demands as well, such as 'a free and liberall contribution for the reliefe of the souldiers', or 'to contribute their old Cloathes … towards the relief of the … poore Souldiers'. Refugees from the fighting elsewhere also headed to London and it became 'a City of refuge and sustaine the distressed and plundered from other parts.'[15] Some Londoners willingly contributed more than their dues to the Parliamentarian cause – in May 1644, *Mercurius Civicus* reported that the 'Maidens of the Parish of Aldermanbury have already raised a compleat Troop of Horse.'[16]

The passage of traffic in and out of London was strictly controlled and in June 1644, Parliament imposed a duty on all goods passing in and out of London. It was the responsibility of those stationed at the various Courts of Guard to stop and search all traffic and prevent the passage of any munitions, unless under the signed warrant of the Speaker of the House of Commons. An exercise duty on a wide range of commodities including beer, cider and meat was introduced, whilst Londoners faced a new demand being made almost every other month: in October 1643 they had to contribute towards the funding of the Scottish army, in February 1644 they contributed towards the upkeep of forces to defend London, and in the following month the value of one meal per week was asked for towards arming the auxiliary regiments. This was in addition to contributions towards the defences themselves; the Parliamentary order of 7 March 1643 specified that inhabitants would contribute towards the construction of the defences at a rate of six pence for houses with a rentable value of five pounds per year and for those with a higher rentable value, two pence in the pound. However, this was still not enough to meet the costs, and in September a Parliamentary ordinance imposed an additional monthly charge.

There was a significant neutral element, and whilst the Royalist threat did temporarily motivate Londoners to come behind Parliament, this was only temporary and conditions in London brought about feelings of war-weariness. The biggest Royalist threat in 1643 and 1644 came not from direct military action but through the disruption of coal shipments, food supplies and trade.[17] *Mercurius Civicus* reported that the 'Cavaliers have plundered most of the Carriers which have gone out from London.'[18] It was later reported that 'the riches and glory thereof is now in a manner wholly destroyed'.

Given this, it is no surprise that the greatest threat to the solidarity of Londoner's support for Parliament came not from the Royalists but from

---

15 *Mercurius Civicus*, Vol. 1, pp. 134–5.
16 *Ibid.*, Vol. 2, p. 113.
17 *The English Civil War – A Contemporary Account*, Vol. 3, p. 81.
18 *Mercurius Civicus*, Vol. 1, p. 165.

neutralism. Although there were no local treaties or the need for a 'third force' to keep the war away from the area, there were calls for peace which continued throughout 1643, occasionally developing into protests, the most notable of which occurred in August 1643 when three days of demonstrations took place.

On 9 August 1643, a multitude (the majority were women who were generally described as 'the wives of substantial citizens or women whose husbands were serving in one army or the other') gathered outside Parliament to protest for peace. They swarmed into Westminster Palace Yard yelling 'Give us those traitors that were against peace!' and 'Give us that dog Pym!' They clashed with the Trained Bands on guard and were only dispersed by a troop of Sir William Waller's cavalry, but angrily vowed their intention to return in greater numbers the next day and threatened to demolish all the new fortifications. According to *Mercurius Civicus*, 'many of those Medears sent to Bridewell', at least one with her hands bound behind her with match.[19] Following this, 'every effort, not omitting violence, is use to purge this city of the pacific Royalists and neutrals'.[20] But it was not only peace protestors wearing white ribbons who took to the streets during the first year of war; there was a vocal pro-war party who were opposed both to the peace protestors and to the moderates within Parliament (and whilst not apparent at the time, it was these hardliners who would come to dominate the political landscape four years later). There were instances where those who wanted peace clashed with those who didn't: in December 1642, the peace protestors were forced to barricade themselves in the Guildhall when attacked by an angry mob. Not long afterwards, several thousand peace protestors took to the streets although this apparent undermining of the Parliamentarian war effort was met with individuals being searched and disarmed.

The poor of Stepney expressed their war-weariness by demolishing part of one of the forts and threatened to pull down adjoining blockhouses. In a similar vein, around Mount Mill fort, so it is recorded, the perpetrators 'intend to seize the forts and outworks to prevent all supplies'.[21] These were desperate times for times for London, which called for desperate measures; with Lord Mayor Penington usurping absolute power – in addition to his civic authority, on 27 October 1643 he took control of the Tower.[22] Morale in London plummeted again the following year when the survivors of the Parliamentarian defeat at Lostwithiel, many of them from the Trained Bands, returned to London having been forced to march from Cornwall. This was a factor the following year when the New Model Army was recruiting and London failed to fulfil its quota.

Despite having halted the tide of Royalist successes by the end of the autumn of 1643, Parliament was desperate for Scottish support and to this end had agreed to the Solemn League and Covenant, which, in September

---

19 *Ibid*., Vol. 1, p. 82. Medea was Euripides' eponymous female character.
20 *The English Civil War – A Contemporary Account*, Vol. 3, p. 88.
21 *Malignants' Treacherous and Bloody Plot against the Parliament and City of London by God's Providence happily prevented* (London, 31 May 1643).
22 *The English Civil War – A Contemporary Account*, Vol. 3, pp. 81, 90.

1643, was to be read to 'severall Parish-Churches in London and Westminster and in the Suburbs'. At the end of 1643, a group of Royalists probably led by Sir Basil Brooke conspired to divide Parliament and the City authorities, and thus preventing the entry of Scotland into the war. His correspondence was discovered and on 6 January 1644 Brooke and his follow conspirators, Master Riley and Master Violet were imprisoned in the Tower, Violet being accused of being a spy.

There were several instances of indiscipline by Parliamentarian troops in London. For instance, on 23 August 1642 Sir William Dugdale noted that a gentleman living in Ratcliffe Highway was 'assaulted by ... [a] company of souldiers ... [who] rifled him of all that was in the house'. In 1643 several Parliamentarian soldiers attempted to burgle a Chamber in Gray's Inn, whilst the following year a house on Clerkenwell Green belonging to a Lady Bullock was attacked by Parliamentary soldiers, who stole 50 pieces of gold, tore five rings from her fingers and wounded one of her servants. A neighbour, Dr. Sibbald, remonstrated with the soldiers from his window, but was shot at for his trouble, three musket bullets narrowly missing his head.

Weary of war, the City pressed Parliament to order Sir Thomas Fairfax and the New Model Army to give battle.[23] The result was the Battle of Naseby, a resounding defeat for the King. Struck by a musket ball (accidently fired by one of his own soldiers) which had driven a piece of his breastplate into his side during the battle, Phillip Skippon, now commander of Parliament's infantry, returned to London for care. Transported in a horse-litter:

> And coming to Islington, a town little more than a mile from London : it pleased the Lord that it should so fall out (to the greater setting forth of his power and providence) that in the said towne a great Mastiffe Dog, on a sddain, ran most fiercely out of a house, fell furiously upon one of the horses that carried the litter, got the horse by the stones behind, made the horse thereby fling and fly about and beat and shke the litter up and down, too and fro, in a most dangerous, shaking the gentleman's sorely wounded body thereby, and really continually to overthrow the litter and greatly endanger the noble gentleman's life; all which while there being no possible means to beat off the dog, or make him leave hold of the horse, till they ran him through with a sword and kill'd him; which as soon as they could they did; and so brought this noble gentleman to his house in Bartholomewes the Great'.[24]

A surgeon removed the pieces of cloth still embedded in the gash, and granted £200 and a house in Westminster by Parliament, by the end of 1645, Skippon was fit for service again.

Skippon was not the only person who had fought at Naseby to enter the capital as, following their defeat, 3,000 Royalist prisoners, including 500 officers, and three carts of wounded were marched through London.[25]

---

23 *Ibid.*, Vol. 3, p. 234.
24 John Vicars, *England's Worthies under whom all the Civill and Bloudy Warres since Anno 1642, to Anno 1647 are related* (London, 1647).
25 *The English Civil War – A Contemporary Account*, Vol. 3, p. 236.

A CITY AT WAR, 1642–46

The Savoy hospital was the first and most significant of all the military hospitals established during the Civil Wars. It has been described as the 'first of the modern hospitals'. (Thomas Fisher Rare Book Library, University of Toronto)

Londoners resented their presence, objecting to the cost, although many of these prisoners volunteered for service in Ireland.[26]

Just two days after the Battle of Edgehill, Parliament passed a bill recognising its duty of care towards soldiers killed or wounded in its service. This duty also applied to their widows and orphans, and in response, in the same year they established a dedicated hospital for the care and treatment of sick and wounded soldiers in the early Tudor 'Hospital of Henry late King of England of the Savoy'. With its river access enabling casualties to be brought in by boat, and nurses, around 12 in number, recruited from among the widows of soldiers, this was the most significant of all the military hospitals established during the Civil Wars, and has been described as the 'first of the modern hospitals'. But by 1645 it was overflowing, and some 1,500 soldiers and widows had to be accommodated elsewhere.[27] The Savoy remained the sole military hospital in London until March 1645 when a second was opened to the west of London. Known as 'Parsons Green', it was actually located at Brandenburgh House, on the river just south of Hammersmith.[28] This catered for soldiers from the armies of the Earls of Essex, Manchester and Denbigh, Sir William Waller, the Trained Bands, and several Royalists. Parsons Green closed at the end of the First Civil War.

Three years later, Ely House was converted from a military prison to a military hospital. From April 1648, treatment was spilt between the Savoy

---

26 House of Commons Journals, Vol. IV, pp. 187, 218.
27 *Ibid.*, Vol. IV, p. 185.
28 *Parliamentary Hospitals in London during the Civil Wars and Interregnum* (London: London Metropolitan Archives, 4 October 2008), pp. 4–5.

and Ely House, with the Savoy concentrating on surgery and Ely House on medical care, although records for October 1648 show that Ely House had filled up in just two to three weeks of its opening. Ely House was also the administrative centre for administration and welfare provision. Whilst the majority of wounded and sick soldiers were cared for at the Savoy, Parsons Green and Ely House, a few were cared for at the existing hospitals at St Bartholomew's (although the Royalist sympathies of the staff resulted in friction with the military patients; it is alleged that on one occasion a sister in the soldiers' ward willed that the head of Sir Thomas Fairfax be displayed on London Bridge[29]) and St Thomas'.

Of the London military hospitals, the Savoy housed the largest number of patients – records for the last week of October 1648, for instance, list 205 soldiers as patients at the Savoy, 112 at Ely House, 45 at St Bartholomew's, and 28 at St Thomas'. Not all treatments could be provided in the London hospitals, and regularly soldiers would be sent away for treatment. Spa water treatment was popular, and between 1647 and 1651, the Savoy and Ely House spent over £3,000 between them sending soldiers to Bath. With the exception of Parsons Green, Parliament's military hospitals lasted until shortly after the Restoration of Charles II.[30] Following their closure, it would be two decades before the Royal Hospitals at Chelsea and Kilmainham (Dublin) would be opened.

The Earl of Essex died at Essex House on 14 September 1646, his death further weakening the Presbyterian faction in Parliament, a faction which had been on the decline since April 1645, when the Self-denying Ordinance was passed, which both led to the formation of the New Model Army and lessened Presbyterian influence in the running of the Parliamentarian forces. Parliament gave him a state funeral, although his hearse was defaced by a fanatic claiming that without repentance, London would go the way of Sodom and Gomorrah. A salute was fired from each of London's forts, and within Westminster Abbey, the chancel was draped in black and a funeral effigy of the Earl in scarlet breeches, a buff-coat and his Parliamentary robes was erected beneath a catafalque designed by Inigo Jones. This was left standing until a former Royalist soldier from Dorset hacked it down on the grounds that an angel had told him to do so. Uniquely, Essex's body was not dug up at the Restoration and so remains with the Abbey.

---

29   *Ibid.*, p. 3.
30   *Ibid.*, pp. 5–6.

5

London's Armaments Industry

Arguably, London's most important contribution to the Parliamentarian war effort was the manufacture and supply of weapons, ammunition, uniforms and other items of military equipment. Whilst still centred on the square-mile of the City itself, by the 1640s, London's armaments industry had expanded fair beyond the city walls.

Gunpowder production originally took place at the Tower, and the nearby Minories although during the 16th century this had moved into the City itself, and then into the suburbs. Access to water was important for the production of gunpowder, both to power the watermills to grind the powder (although horse power was also used), and to transport the raw materials and finished product. Whilst there were the official government gunpowder stores at the Tower of London and at Greenwich, there were gunpowder 'houses' in Fleet Street and Fetter Lane. Given the obvious dangers of producing gunpowder in urban areas – for example, in 1639, the Office of Ordnance received reports of one Robert Davies storing the ingredients of gunpowder in his Thames Street house, no doubt reported by nervous neighbours since Davies had previously blown up his house in Whitechapel[1] – by the middle of the 17th century production had moved to outlying districts such as Bedfont, Hounslow (there was a gunpowder mill just west of Hounslow Heath, which had been converted from Benjamin Stone's earlier sword factory[2]), and most importantly, the River Lea. Based initially at Stratford, by the end of the 1650s this had spread as far north as Enfield, causing the curate of Waltham Abbey, Dr. Thomas Fuller to write in the 1660s 'more is made by the mills of late erected on the river Lea, betwixt Waltham and London than in all England besides'.[3]

Whilst gunfounding at the Tower of London had declined by the 1620s, this wasn't the end of cannon production in London. Limited production occurred in Finsbury (there was a foundry on what is now Worship Street), whilst in Lambeth in 1629, Charles I allowed Robert Scott to set up a facility

---
1   Wayne D. Cocroft, *Dangerous Energy* (Swindon: English Heritage, 2000), p. 13.
2   David Blackmore, *Arms and Armour of the English Civil War* (London: Royal Armouries, 1990), p. 6.
3   Cocroft, p. 16.

CIVIL WAR LONDON

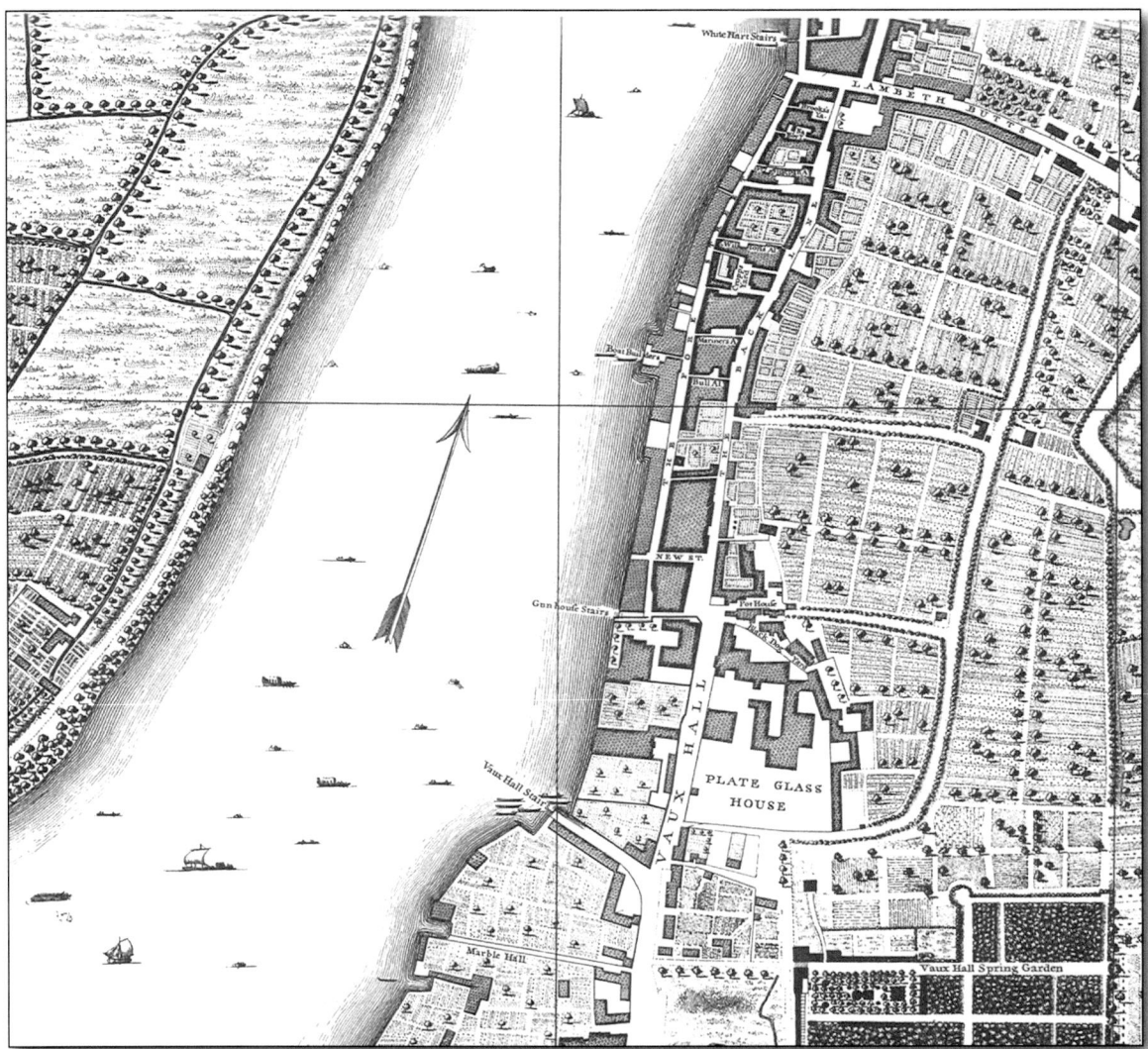

An extract from John Rocque's 1747 map of London. The location of the Copt Hall foundry is marked by 'Gun-house stairs', whilst the remains of Vauxhall Fort (a bastion and a short length of rampart) can be seen at the lower centre of the map. (David Flintham)

for artillery development. Scott had developed the leather gun, a lightweight cannon comprising of a reinforced copper tube encased in leather, in Sweden. This facility was almost certainly at Copt Hall (Faux Hall / Vauxhall). It was a two acre site, dominated by a mansion house. The facilities included two forges and a great forge, a workshop for boring cannon, a new boring room, and a wash house. This would have enabled Faux Hall to both cast and bore ordnance. But most intriguingly, there was also a room where design models were kept.[4] Contemporary descriptions suggest that ordnance at the lighter end of the spectrum, including leather guns and frames (another type of light artillery, typically multi-barrelled) of brass, and possibly musket barrels may have been manufactured there. The London foundries tended to produce the more expensive 'brass' (bronze) ordnance, whilst iron cannon were produced in larger quantities in such places as the Kent and Sussex Weald.

---

4   The National Archives (TNA): SP 28/139 Pt 10 ff. 108–11.

On Scott's death in 1631, Copt Hall passed to James Wemyss, who later supplied light artillery to both Essex and Waller's armies (the Royalist newspaper *Mercurius Aulicus*, says the Parliamentary artillery captured at Cropredy Bridge in June 1644 included 'leather guns [which] were invented by Col Weems, a Scot, who lately made them at Lambeth'.[5] It is also likely that Wemyss supplied guns to Parliamentarian regional armies, and possibly to the London Trained Bands as well.[6] By the autumn of 1643, Wemyss himself was no longer producing cannon at Copt Hall (by this time he was in command of Waller's artillery train), although it is likely that it was still being used for this purpose at least as late as 1647, when Charles I granted the site to William Lambert who, it is recorded, was solely concerned with casting cannon.[7] By the end of the 1640s, however, the site's principle function was as a home for 'Artists, Mechanics &c. and a depot for models and philosophical apparatus'. Sold by Parliament in 1652, who had no use for it as a gun foundry, the site ultimately came into the possession of the inventor, the 2nd Marquis of Worcester. His *Century of Inventions* of 1655 detailed more than 100 inventions, including several connected with firearms and cannon, including a way to keep cannon cool after firing, and a quick-loading gun.[8] In addition, he describes a device, based around a cannon barrel, which would have been one of the earliest steam engines.

A pair of leather guns possibly similar to the type produced at Copt Hall. (David Flintham)

The Museum of London holds the surviving contracts for the provision of uniforms, arms and equipment to the New Model Army for the period April 1645 to March 1646, and this archive demonstrates the importance of London's industries to Parliament's military successes.[9] During 1645–46, the first year of the New Model Army's existence, expenditure on equipment (but not food and accommodation) was £117,000, the vast majority of this on contracts awarded to around 200 London suppliers who were, apparently, paid promptly. There were some instances where the suppliers were existing employees of the Office of Ordinance at the Tower, an obvious conflict of interest.

These orders included gunpowder, musket and cannon shot, granados (mortar shells) and match. Then there were the firearms themselves, and pikes and swords.[10] There were shoes and every item of uniform clothing (the order of 14 February 1645 specifies 'a red colour', with the cloth coming

---

5   *Mercurius Aulicus*, ending 29 June 1644. Oxford, p. 1056.
6   TNA: SP28/139 Pt 10 ff. 108–112.
7   Charles Ffoulkes, *The Gun-Founders of England* (London: Arms and Armour Press, 1969), pp. 52–53.
8   *Ibid*, pp. 53–54.
9   G. I. Mungeam, 'Contracts for the supply of equipment to the "New Model" Army in 1645', *The Journal of the Arms & Armour Society*, vol. VI, no. 3, September 1968, pp. 53–115.
10 Peter Edwards, *Dealing in Death: The Arms Trade and the British Civil Wars, 1638–52* (Stroud: Sutton Publishing Limited, 2000), pp. 95–96.

from Suffolk, Coventry or Gloucestershire[11]). Drums, ensigns, partizans and halberds were also ordered, as was hardware of every kind, including tools, wagon spares, horseshoes and nails. Orders placed on 26 June 1645 totalled 700 saddles, 1,350 pairs of pistols, 900 sets of back and breast armour, 800 helmets and 500 holsters. The majority of the equipment ordered was delivered directly to the Tower of London for onward supply to the army. Whilst the majority of the suppliers were still within the Square Mile, firearm production took place close to the Tower in St Katherine's, the Minories and in East Smithfield, whilst saddlery was being made in Whitechapel and Radcliffe, and in Southwark. The army commissariats' requirements went beyond clothing, footwear, arms, ammunition and saddlery: food and drink, and a range of other goods and services were also required, such as rope makers, coopers, vintners, apothecaries, surgeons, and carters. Then there was the supply of horses: although there were several dealers based in Smithfield, and the New Model Army did issue a number of warrants to purchase horses from them, horses were normally obtained locally, whilst on campaign.

Impressive as these orders are, some caution needs to be exercised. Was London's role principally as a producer of this equipment rather than an importer and distributor? Certainly some of the orders do suggest that the actual manufacture took place elsewhere (ordnance from the Weald of Kent, swords from Birmingham, and shoes from Northampton for instance), and the response of London's gunmakers and cutlers during the Bishops' Wars was sluggish: therefore had these industries had time to develop into large-scale arms manufacturing four years later? But by the early 17th century, manufacturing occupied 40 percent of the workforce, with clothing being the dominant industry. By the 1640s, leather working and metal working (the latter was increasing in its share of the market) was prominent in the suburbs, particularly to the east. Therefore, London should be seen as being at the heart of supply to Parliament's armies, both as a producer and as an importer and distributor.

---

11   Mungeam, pp. 68–69.

6

Counter-revolution, 1646–49

By the summer of 1647, Jacob Astley's prophetic words spoken after his defeat at Stow-on-the-Wold the previous year ('You have done your work, boys, and may go play, unless you will fall out among yourselves') were beginning to come true, as divisions began to emerge between the victorious New Model Army and their radical 'Independent' supporters in Parliament on one side and the 'Presbyterian' party at Westminster on the other. In February 1647 the Presbyterian party, who wanted to come to moderate terms with the King, moved to disband the New Model Army, in so doing, denying it arrears of pay. Thus a showdown between the army and its parliamentary opponents was inevitable. In June, the army seized the King, removing him from Parliament's custody, and held him at Hampton Court. The Army Council put new relatively moderate peace terms, the Heads of the Proposals, to the King. But Charles dismissed these, hoping that he could use the discord between the Independent party and the Army on one side and the Presbyterian party, the City of London and its militia on the other to his own ends. Looking back over five years of civil war, it is important to remember that those considered 'radical' in 1642 were not necessarily radical in 1647: some were supporters of the Presbyterians and so may be considered 'moderate', others were more hardline and supported the trial and execution of the King, whilst others, more radical still, supported the Levellers, the most popular and thus well-known radical movement of the period.

On 22 July, the Independents voted to disband the Presbyterian-dominated City of London Militia Committee, but in response, a mob (probably including Cavaliers, inciting the others) descended on Parliament, demanding the reinstatement of the committee and the unconditional return of the King. This was exploited (perhaps even instigated) by some Presbyterian MPs and by the City authorities who now planned to raise an army to defend what was evolving into a counter-revolution against the Army and its supporters in Parliament. This 'defence force' was to be commanded by Sir William Waller, Sydenham Poyntz, and Edward Massey, each very experienced Parliamentarian generals. It was comprised of 'reformadoes' (soldiers from disbanded Parliamentarian regiments not brought in the New Model), deserters from the New Model, but chiefly London's militia itself.

CIVIL WAR LONDON

The Cromwell Association's memorial to the Putney Debates, St Mary's Church. (David Flintham)

The Independents fled, and sought the protection of the Army, thus giving the Army the excuse it needed to seize control of the capital. On 4 August, at his headquarters on Hounslow Heath, the army's commander-in-chief, Sir Thomas Fairfax, met with representatives of the City's Court of Common Council, who had, by now, lost the will to resist, and promptly capitulated, ordering the Trained Bands to withdraw from London's fortifications. Two days later Fairfax marched into London at the head of 16,000 troops – the line of troops stretching for nearly a mile and a half. The line of march resembled a victory parade: the soldiers wore laurel sprigs in their caps as a symbol of victory. The City authorities had attempted to install fear and apprehension within its citizens that following in the wake of the New Model army would be plunder and rapine,[1] but such was the exemplary behaviour of the soldiers; their passage through the City on 7 August was cheered. Fairfax, having occupied the capital unopposed, now proceeded to restore the Independent MPs to parliament. He then turned his attention to the City, having the Mayor, one of the sheriffs and three aldermen arrested and imprisoned in the Tower. He gave the control of the Militia Committee to Independents and then set about ordering the demolition of London's fortifications with pretext that their removal would ease the financial burden on Londoners. On 26 August the Army established its headquarters in Putney, close enough to London to be able to put pressure on Parliament should the need arise, and also to prevent hostile forces being raised, but far enough away so as not to be too intimidating. The Army's headquarters were to remain at Putney (then a rural village, some four miles upstream from Westminster) until 17 November 1647.

The apparent discipline of the Army hid the cracks which were now beginning to appear in its unity, as within its ranks was a growing Leveller element. The Levellers emphasised popular sovereignty, extended suffrage, common land ownership, equality before the law, and religious tolerance, and probably did more than any other single group to bring about the Republic in 1649. Whilst the movement was not restricted to the capital, London was its incubator and its mainstay. Although radicalism was present in several parishes across London (particularly in Southwark and Wapping), and there were a number of churches, and inns, taverns and alehouses where radicals congregated (one contemporary describing the latter as 'the Devil's castles'), Coleman Street was London's radical heart.

Thus, the Army's Levellers now gained strength from the Levellers in London and their constitutional demands were something that its senior officers, the Grandees, would not tolerate. That the Grandees were also seeking an accommodation with the King only widened these divisions.

---

1   BL, Thomason Tracts, E400-(35), *Eighteen Queries* (2 August 1647).

On 28 October 1647, the Army Council met in St Mary's Church in Putney. What became known as the Putney Debates were chaired by Lieutenant General Oliver Cromwell and was attended by both senior officers and Leveller agitators. The debates went on for 10 days, and despite the celebrated exchange between the Leveller Colonel Thomas Rainsborough and the Grandee, Henry Ireton, the outcome was very much in favour of the Grandees.[2]

During the final months of 1647, the divide between Presbyterian and Independent, and Parliament and Army grew ever wider, as all sides attempted to find their own solution as to what to do with the King. Elsewhere there were pockets of unrest which would ultimately boil over into renewed fighting. One of a number of triggers was the banning of Christmas; whilst as early as 1643, some London shops remained open on Christmas Day, it was not until 1647 that Christmas Day was officially abolished. Londoners defied the ban by decorating churches with rosemary and bay, whilst a pump in Cornhill was decorated by London apprentices in holly and ivy. There were suspicions of a Royalist conspiracy in London[3] and unrest elsewhere (there was a serious riot in Canterbury, for instance), and by the spring of 1648, this popular protest turned pro-Royalist: on 31 March, the anniversary of the King's accession, bonfires were lit in the streets of London and passers-by were forced to drink the King's health. The following month the authorities attempted to stop children playing games and the apprentices protested against this overreaction. In response, Colonel Rich's and Colonel Barkstead's regiments of New Model horse and foot respectively intervened and two apprentices were killed. The next day, the apprentices took the City gates at Ludgate and Newgate, and in in response, troops surrounded the City walls and then marched through Moorgate against the protesters, killing some, capturing others although most were dispersed.

On 16 May there was further unrest as Surrey petitioners marched through the City shouting 'For God and King Charles'. In the ensuing 'scuffle', one or two soldiers were killed,[4] and then the protest moved to the House of Commons where they were met by Rich's and Barkstead's regiments, which were by then deployed in Whitehall and the Mews,[5] who killed several protesters. In response to this perceived 'heavy-handedness' by the Army, they were persuaded to remove its garrison from the Tower, the City installing its militia in its place.

On 21 May, rebellion broke out in Kent, and five days later, Royalist sympathisers from Southwark marched on Deptford. The London Trained Bands were given responsibility for guarding the Houses of Parliament,

---

2 Not only was Wapping-born Rainsborough a leading Leveller, he was also Parliament's 'siege-master'. He began his Parliamentary service at sea, and in January 1648 was appointed vice admiral. But his radical views were unpopular and resulted in the mutiny which was one of the causes of the Second Civil War.
3 *The English Civil War – Contemporary Account*, Vol. 3, p. 356.
4 Ibid., Vol. 4, p. 22.
5 Ian Gentles, 'The struggle for London in the Second Civil War', *Historical Journal*, 1983; Gentles, *The New Model Army in England, Ireland, and Scotland 1645–1653* (Oxford: Blackwell, 1992), p. 246.

Sir Thomas Fairfax, commander of the New Model Army. (Thomas Fisher Rare Book Library, University of Toronto)

which allowed Rich's regiment of horse and some companies of Barkstead's foot to secure Southwark. The next day, Fairfax reviewed his troops on Hounslow Heath, and the Royalist insurgents abandoned Deptford and headed to Dartford. On 29 May the Earl of Norwich was proclaimed leader of the Kent Royalists, but the following day the arrival of Fairfax at Blackheath forced the Dartford insurgents to disperse. On 1 June, Fairfax defeated the Kentish Royalists at Maidstone, and whilst the majority of them dispersed, about 3,000 remained with Norwich and headed towards London. Pursued by a party of horse and dragoons commanded by Colonel Whalley, Norwich reached Blackheath on 3 June, where he discovered that the gates of London were barred against him and the City resolutely defended by Skippon and the London Trained Bands. The following day, with most of his followers deserting him, news of a Royalist uprising in Essex prompted Norwich to cross the Thames at Greenwich to seek out the Essex Royalists. Sir William Compton crossed the Thames with 500 Royalist cavalry, and had the better of the skirmishes around Bow Bridge,[6] which allowed them to head first to Chelmsford and ultimately to Colchester.

Elsewhere in the country there were armed uprisings, and the Navy mutinied. A Royalist fleet under the command of the Prince Wales positioned itself for a while in the Thames estuary, temporarily disrupting London's trade once more.[7] The King, whilst he had been negotiating with Parliament, had entered into a secret engagement with the Scots, who invaded England in the summer of 1648. As widespread as these outbreaks were, they were not coordinated which meant that could each be defeated in turn. The short but bloody Second Civil War proved to many that the King could not be trusted, yet by the autumn of 1648, Parliament reopened negotiations with Charles. This was the final straw. In early winter, the army moved the King to Windsor and then marched on London.

Thus is the space of just over a year, the New Model Army had twice marched on London, events witnessed by the teenage Samuel Pepys. Londoners were overawed by this show of strength; whilst the army was under strict instructions to 'demean themselves civilly and peaceably', there could be no mistaking that this was an army of occupation. On the morning

---

6   Robert Monteth, *The History of the Troubles of Great Britain* (London: A. Millar, 1738), pp. 421–22, and Matthew Carter, *A True relation of that honourable, though unfortunate expedition of Kent, Essex and Colchester in 1648* (Colchester: J. Marsden, 1810), pp. 48–50.
7   *The English Civil War – A Contemporary Account*, Vol. 4, pp. 29–30.

of 6 December 1648, the Trained Bands marched to Whitehall to take up their usual position guarding Parliament only to find their way blocked by the New Model Army. Under the command of Colonel Thomas Pride, the army purged the House of Commons of any opposition (some 100 MPs were excluded, including 45 who were actually arrested – others prudently removed themselves). It was the remaining 'Rump' of around 70 MPs who would address the matter of bringing the King to trial.

On 1 January 1649 the Rump Parliament passed an ordinance for the trial of the King which commenced on the 20th in Westminster Hall (although the evidence was heard in the Painted Chamber rather than Westminster Hall). On the 26 the King was condemned as a 'tyrant, traitor, murderer and public enemy to the Commonwealth of England', and the next day, the President of the Court, John Bradshaw, pronounced the death sentence. Charles, who had acted with quiet dignity throughout the proceedings, to his great dismay was not allowed to speak and was abruptly led away from the court by soldiers, further emphasising the overriding presence of the Army in the proceedings, to await his execution. Thus by January 1649, the triumph of Cromwell and the Independents over both the King, and the Presbyterians in Parliament, was virtually complete.

7

The Commonwealth Capital, 1649–58

Soon after nine o'clock in the morning of 30 January 1649, Charles I was taken from St James's Palace by two companies of infantry and crossed St James's Park to the Banqueting House, Whitehall. As the arrangements for the execution were still not complete, Charles was forced to wait until early afternoon in the room which had once been his bedchamber, when Colonel Hacker came for the King; he took him up the staircase leading to the first floor and out of a window onto the scaffold, which had been erected against the wall of a now demolished brick extension to the north of the Banqueting House. Richard Brandon, who had executed the Earl of Strafford in 1641, was, in all likelihood, also the executioner of Charles I. Pepys, aged 15 and strongly republican, witnessed the execution of Charles I, recalling that following the event two troops of soldiers moved from either end of what is now Whitehall to disperse the crowd.

On 9 March, several Royalists captured during the Second Civil War (including the Earl of Holland and Lord Capel) were beheaded in Westminster, and in the same month, Lord Mayor Abraham Reynardson was fined £2,000, and imprisoned in the Tower of London for two months for refusing to make public the Act proclaiming the abolition of the kingly office. He was also deposed from the mayoralty.

In March 1649, a disillusioned John Lilburne, the leader of the Leveller movement and thorn in the side of Cromwell, wrote 'We were before ruled by King, Lords and Commons, now by a General, a Court Martial, and House of Commons: and we pray you what is the difference?' Soon afterwards, prominent Levellers, Lilburne, William Walwyn, Richard Overton and Thomas Price, were imprisoned in the Tower on a charge of treason. This was followed by a mutiny by 30 men in Colonel Whalley's regiment. Six were sentenced to death and whilst five were pardoned; one, Robert Lockyer, was executed by firing squad in St Paul's Cathedral churchyard. For radical Londoners he became a martyr; some 4,000, many defiantly wearing Leveller symbols, attended his funeral at the New Churchyard (also known as the Bethlem Burial Ground) in April. Women, the 'lusty lasses of the levelling party', campaigned for Lilburne's release and laid siege to the House of

Commons for three days. Whilst Lilburne was later acquitted of the charges brought against him and freed from the Tower, he went into exile. Returning from exile in 1653, he was immediately arrested and imprisoned in Newgate. He was tried and acquitted (troops filled London during the trial, but despite the efforts of their officers, the news of Lilburne's acquittal was greeted with shouts and the sounds of trumpets). Arrested again, he was imprisoned in Newgate, then the Tower, before being sent to Jersey, and then Dover Castle. But soon afterwards, with his health failing, and his spirit broken, he gave up the Leveller struggle and become a Quaker. Following his death in Eltham on 29 August 1657, and was buried at the New Churchyard.

Following the execution of the King, the House of Commons abolished the Monarchy and the House of Lords, declaring that the people of England 'to be henceforth under the governance of a "Commonwealth". For the first two years of the Commonwealth, the Rump, dependent on the support of the Army (an uneasy relationship) faced economic depression and the risk of invasion from Scotland and Ireland. By 1653, with the Third Civil War won, the threat from both Scotland and Ireland had been removed. But the end of the Civil Wars did not bring about a period of peace for the Cromwellian Commonwealth. Whilst there were Royalist uprisings (1653–54, 1655 and 1659), more significantly for London were the 'foreign' wars, against the Dutch (1652–54), and Spain (1654–59). The latter was part of the Franco-Spanish War and involved England from the summer of 1654 when an expeditionary forced was dispatched to the Caribbean, and between 1657–59 when Cromwellian troops, allied with France, fought against Royalist troops, who were allied with Spain. Whilst removed from the actual fighting, London did see its hospitals used to treat the wounded, and its prisons to hold the captured. The forces sent to Flanders in 1657 mustered on Blackheath before their departure to France.

On 20 April 1653, Cromwell, assisted by Thomas Harrison, forcibly dismissed the Rump (thus proving correct the fears that Parliament would be abolished and government would be in the hands of a council appointed by the Army). The Rump was replaced by so-called Barebone's Parliament, named after one of its members, Praise-God Barebone, a freeman of the Leathersellers' Company, and a lay preacher to a congregation who worshipped at his warehouse, the Lock and Key in Fleet Street. Whilst the radical minority raged against the government from the pulpits of St Anne's, Blackfriars, Allhallows-the-Great in Upper Thames Street, and Christ Church Newgate, Cromwell's personal power was further strengthened in December 1653 when he was installed as Lord Protector. He enjoyed the support of London and, of course, the Army, but not always the support of the Navy: on

John Lilburne, the leader of the Levellers.

CIVIL WAR LONDON

The execution of Charles I on 30 January 1649, outside the Banqueting Hall, Whitehall.

26 October 1653, Cromwell and General-at-Sea, George Monck were accosted by thousands of sailors in Whitehall, angry that their pay was outstanding. Monck dispersed them, preventing any of the sailors being taken as rioters.[1] Cromwell made a formal state visit to the City in February 1654, knighting the Mayor, Thomas Viner.[2] Whilst there were still grumblings among the citizenry and from a number of Independents, the bulk of the population came to accept the Protectorate and its quasi-royal status. During the spring of 1654, what remained of the old royal residences of St James's, Whitehall, Somerset House, Greenwich and Hampton Court were retrieved (a process which was complicated and expensive given the method of their disposal after January 1649[3]), and placed at the disposal of the Lord Protector.

There was further political unrest in 1655 when the talk was whether Cromwell would accept the crown, the government hoping to suppress dissent by controlling places where people might meet: thus they attempted to close alehouses, gaming houses, bawdy houses and theatres. The threat was no longer just from Royalists, and now Republicans came under suspicion and many were imprisoned. In August of that year, Cromwell embarked on a process of direct military rule (at the end of 1654, there were approximately 23,000 troops stationed in Ireland, 19,000 in Scotland and 11,000 in England, a total of 53,000), dividing the country into 11 regions, each governed by a major general who answered to the Lord Protector. The major general for London was Phillip Skippon, but given his age, the day-to-day responsibility fell to his deputy, Major General John Barkstead. The rule of the Major Generals lasted until January 1657.

Royalist support never completely disappeared from London, but the system of compounding – the fining of Royalists – ensured those who remained were faced with a heavy financial burden. There were occasional outbreaks of pro-Royalist graffiti, but even when there was organised Royalist resistance – the Sealed Knot was formed in November 1653 – it proved to be disappointingly ineffective. The Royalists' lack of organisation made the

---

1   Peter Reese, *The Life of General George Monck* (Barnsley: Pen and Sword Books Limited, 2008), p. 92.
2   *The English Civil War – A Contemporary Account*, Vol. 4, pp. 175–77.
3   *Ibid*, Vol. 4, p. 55.

THE COMMONWEALTH CAPITAL, 1649–58

Members of the English Civil War Society commemorate the anniversary of the execution of King Charles I, an annual event which takes place on the last Sunday in January. (David Flintham)

job of John Thurloe, the head of government intelligence, that much easier. Another area in which the state exercised tight control was propaganda. The 1640s and 50s saw such an outpouring of printed material that the period is generally acknowledged to have marked the birth of the popular press, yet by the middle of the 1650s tighter censorship by the Protectorate government meant that Marchamont Needham's *Mercurius Politicus* and his *Public Intelligencer* were virtually the only publications in regular circulation.

The army did not come cheap and the Commonwealth government continually looked for ways to raise funds. In 1652, Hyde Park was sold by order of Parliament, but the following year, as John Evelyn noted, 'the sordid fellow' who had purchased part of the park, was charging 1s for every coach and 6d for every horse to enter it. May Day 1654 'was more observed by people going a-maying than for divers years past. Great resort came to Hyde Park, many hundreds of rich coaches and gallants in attire but most shameful powdered hair, main painted and spotted women. But his Highness the Lord Protector went not thither nor any of the Lords of the Council.' Also popular at the time were coach races, and on one occasion Cromwell himself:

> Provoked the horses [so much] with the whip that they grew unruly and ran so fast that the postilion could not hold them in whereby His Highness [Cromwell] was flung out of the coachbox upon the pole, on which he lay with his body and afterwards fell upon the ground. His foot getting hold of the tackling, he was carried away a good while in that posture during which time a pistol went off in his pocket. But at last he got his foot clear and so came to escape.

In the same month Peter Vowell, a schoolmaster from Islington, was arrested for his part in a plot to assassinate Cromwell. Vowell was supposedly to provide arms and help seize the troopers' horses while they grazed in Islington fields. Forewarned, the authorities arrested the plotters and after questioning, three of the conspirators were put on trial. On 30 June they were found guilty of treason and on 10 July Vowell was hanged at Charing Cross. Of the other conspirators, Gerard was beheaded at Tower Hill and Fox, having confessed, was transported to Barbados the following year. The Royalist threat, especially at the time of the Penruddock Rising in March 1655, was viewed significant enough that the garrison of the Tower of London was increased to 1,200 men and a battery of cannon was sited at what is now Horse Guards Parade in Whitehall. The Venetian ambassador felt that the majority of the population of London were conspiring against the 'despotic Cromwell', noting that soldiers were regularly being posted along several of London's streets to keep the population in check,[4] and Thurloe commenced a round-up of leading Royalists. On 6 July 1655, a proclamation ordered Royalists to leave London, and those who had fought for the King were not allowed to come within 20 miles of the Capital.[5] Cromwell's government proved itself to be equally adept at seeing off a renewed Republican threat, and during the first two months of 1658 Cromwell had called, and dissolved, the second Protectorate Parliament. His power seemed absolute. In May 1658, another Royalist plot was uncovered – Thurloe was kept well informed of the conspirators 'secret' meetings at the 'Feathers' in Cheapside. Of the conspirators, two, Henry Slingsby and Doctor Hewitt, the latter an Anglican clergyman from St Gregory's by St Pauls, were beheaded on Tower Hill, whilst a further three were hung drawn and quartered – a rare example of the traditional penalty for treason being carried out in Cromwell's England. These executions were sure to have drawn a crowd, as Tyburn executions were a popular sight. In June 1649 for example, a crowd of many thousands witnessed the execution of 24 people at the same time, whilst on Whit Monday 1651, Phillip Powell and Peter Wright along with 13 other felons were executed in front of a crowd of more than 20,000. On 12 April 1652, Joan Peterson, 'the Wapping Witch', was executed.

The religious 'settlement' of the 1650s affected the different religious groups in varying ways. Whilst the government was primarily Independent, Presbyterianism was still strong, particularly amongst the middle and gentry classes, and within the City of London where the rigid discipline of the presbyters offered a defence against the dangerous democratic notion of the Independent sects, several of which were based in London. Whilst the great majority of the Independent congregations existed quite happily in Republican England, there were limits, most notably towards the Quakers. But often either toleration or persecution was down to local administration rather than Government policy. But whilst Cromwell famously readmitted the Jews into England, there was no place in the Commonwealth's broad church for

---

4   *Ibid.*, Vol. 4, pp. 187–91.
5   *Ibid.*, Vol. 4, p. 263.

Catholics or Episcopalian Anglicans. The new Directory of Worship proved to be even more unpopular that the Book of Common Prayer it replaced, and whilst the fabric of the church suffered at the hands of the iconoclasts, many Anglicans, John Evelyn amongst them, were driven underground.

But the London of the 1650s was not a completely cheerless city. Taverns and cookhouses were popular places for Londoners to socialise (Pepys enjoyed card games, musical evenings and gambling), and in 1656 it was recorded that there were 1,153 drinking establishments in London, ranging from basic alehouses (the equivalent of today's pubs), through middling taverns (today's restaurants), to more upmarket inns (modern day hotels). Drunkenness was a social problem as was the so-called 'dry-drunkenness' caused by tobacco smoking. The Major Generals attempted to control alehouses and in London, all landlords were warned that they would lose their licences if they profaned the Sabbath or allowed games to be played on their premises.

In 1652, coffee drinking came to London, introduced by Daniel Edwards, a merchant who traded with Turkey and had acquired the habit of taking coffee in the mornings. The proprietor, Pasqua Rosée, was the servant of Edwards who imported the coffee and assisted Rosée in setting up the establishment. The coffee house, which opened in 1652, is known in some accounts as The Turk's Head. Chocolate was first advertised in the same year, whilst in 1658, tea was advertised in *Mercurius Politicus*. The coffee house soon became a popular place for Londoners to meet and discuss topical issues and politics. James Harrington, an Oxford educated lawyer, founded the Rota, a Republican-influenced political debating society. Meeting at the Turk's Head Coffee House in Westminster's New Palace Yard, its membership included Samuel Pepys.

The Commonwealth's attitude to the seedier side of London life was decidedly intolerant. The Blasphemy Act was passed in 1650, and the acts that this moral code sought to outlaw included swearing which was now subject to fines, whilst adultery was made a felony with the death penalty for the second conviction. But ultimately this proved to be too draconian for even Puritan juries. In the spring of 1656, Major General John Barkstead carried out a sweep of the London brothels, transporting 'many loose wenches' to Jamaica and arresting others for running bawdy houses. But despite this, the campaign against sexual immorality remained patchy and ineffectual. Parliament's clampdown on theatres was only partially successful, and theatres continued to stage performances although with the constant threat that they would be raided and actors arrested. Whilst theatre performances were banned during the 1640s, it was not until 1656 that animal sports were outlawed

1650s London was overcrowded and it was dirty: pollution was a problem even then. But as the City's population grew, its infrastructure developed to keep pace, and by mid-century, travel within and outside the capital improved. The Thames remained a popular thoroughfare, however, with wherries – the 17th century equivalent of modern river-buses – running regular passenger services. Land transport also improved, and during the 1640s the hackney carriage appeared (from the Old French word 'haquenée', meaning an ambling horse) and in 1654 Parliament passed an Act requiring London's Aldermen to license the City's hackney carriages. By the end of the 1650s, stage coaches were operating regular services on all the main routes out of London, although it took two days to reach Oxford (compared with a day on horseback[6]), four to Chester and six to Edinburgh. Whilst it was the reign of Charles I that the first public mail service was introduced, the office of Postmaster General increased in importance during the Commonwealth, and from 1662 the carrying of letters was declared to be a monopoly of the King, effectively marking the beginning of the Royal Mail.

---

6   John Barratt, *Cavalier Capital: Oxford in the English Civil War 1642–1646* (Solihull: Helion & Company, 2015), p. 21.

8

The Return of the King, 1658–60

In early September 1658, a great storm raged across southern England, which was, according to Clarendon 'the greatest storm of wind that had ever known … which overthrew trees, houses and made great wrecks at sea.'[1] Oliver Cromwell died on 3 September, and it was said by his enemies that the storm that had wracked havoc across southern England was the Devil carrying away Cromwell's soul. The Puritan ethic had reduced baptisms and marriages to simple, civil affairs, and whilst elaborate funerals and ostentatious displays of mourning were condemned, Cromwell's funeral in 1658 was lavish, costing £60,000 (including a £4,000 hearse). The funeral took place on 23 November (it had to be postponed from 9 November due to the length of time the preparations took), although Cromwell's body had actually been privately buried earlier. From Somerset House where Cromwell had lain in state, the funeral procession proceeded along the Strand and then along King Street and Whitehall to Westminster Abbey. Yet most of those present must of known that Cromwell's body had already been buried since, as John Evelyn noted, that whilst there were 'innumerable mourners', 'there was none that Cried', and even the soldiers lining the route of the funeral were seen drinking and taking tobacco.

Cromwell was succeeded as Lord Protector by his son, Richard. The City was more unanimous for Cromwell, 'Tumbledown Dick', than it had been for his father, yet he was a reluctant successor and on 8 June 1659, he abdicated. In his stead was the Rump Parliament, the residue of the Long Parliament of nearly 20 years before. On 13 October, the Republican Major General John Lambert staged a military coup, and ejected the speaker and most of the MPs from Parliament. But this army junta lasted only until December when the army leaders fell out amongst themselves, and the politicians returned. Meanwhile, in Scotland, General Monck, who had distanced himself from the army junta, had moved his troops to the border, but despite the City

---

[1] Edward, Earl of Clarendon, *The History of the Rebellion and Civil Wars in England* (Oxford: The Clarendon Press, 1826), vol. 7, p. 292.

George Monck, commander-in-chief in Scotland and instrumental in the Restoration of Charles II.

Council asking him for his support, Monck's intentions were yet unknown.

Troops again returned to London's streets, added to which Vice Admiral Lawson had brought his fleet to the Thames estuary and threatened to blockade London, cutting off the supply of coal and corn. And so chaos returned: in December 1659 another riot by apprentices caused shops to be boarded up, and was met by the army who fired into the crowd, killing two. In response, Londoners barred the gates at Temple Bar, and whilst the officer commanding the soldiers was indicted for murder, there were repeated calls for the Army to leave the capital. Thus the City Council, the Rump, Lambert, Monck, and Lawson each had their own objectives, whilst in the background, the Royalists plotted. Many felt that the country was descending into its fourth civil war.

The year 1659 ended in an atmosphere of general alarm and despondency, but help was on its way, ironically, considering where the Civil Wars had started, from Scotland. On 2 January 1660 (the day after Pepys started writing his diary), Monck acted. In what Thomas Hobbes was to describe as 'the greatest stratagem that is extant in history',[2] Monck crossed the River Tweed at Coldstream and led his army, his 'Coldstreamers', south towards London; Lambert's on force disintegrated in its path. But as Monck marched south, he received the alarming news that the troops currently based in London outnumbered his own. From St Albans, he wrote to William Lenthall, Speaker of the House of Commons, requesting that, with the exception of two regiments, they were to be sent to new quarters across the country. Despite the objections of republicans like Sir Arthur Hesilrige, the House of Commons decided it had no option but to comply. However, as Monck neared London, one of the regiments, commanded by the son of the Speaker, refused to leave the capital. But the dispatch of some cavalry by Monck easily suppressed the disturbance, despite that fact that it was supported by some apprentices.

The morning of 3 February 1660 found Monck's small army in Highgate. From there it commenced its ceremonial march into London, proceeding down Gray's Inn Lane to Holborn, before heading along Fleet Street, through Temple Bar and then along the Strand. Londoners, who had seen more than enough soldiers over recent years, were not initially enthusiastic about having yet another army marching through the capital; but the Coldstreamers were different: one eyewitness commented, 'Their Scotch horse were thin and out of case with long hard Marching; and the men as rough and weather beaten,

---

2   Hobbes, *Behemoth*, p. 204.

having marched in a severe Winter about three hundred Mile in length, and through deep and continued Snows.'[3] The strict discipline of the army won at least some Londoners over, and Monck was greeted by the ringing of church bells, and from where he stood in the Strand, Pepys counted 31 bonfires lit in celebration. Pausing to be formally welcomed at Somerset House, the army then resumed its march to Whitehall. Appointing officers loyal to him to command the two remaining London regiments, Monck now had London under military control. Without proper barracks in London, the Coldstreamers were quartered in pubs and inns in Clerkenwell and Islington.

Yet there was no indication which way Monck would turn. Would he favour the existing Rump Parliament, or call for the expelled Members to return to Parliament, or for the restoration of the Monarchy? And so the uncertainty continued. There were calls for a free Parliament from the City, and the Rump, concerned that such demands would escalate into protest or worse, ordered Monck into the City to destroy its barriers, portcullises and gates. Initially, albeit reluctantly, Monck complied, but within days, he had decided, or had been persuaded by his officers, that since the Rump had not taken the opportunity to reform itself he would join the calls for a free Parliament. Taken by surprise, the Rump reacted by replacing Monck with Charles Fleetwood as commander-in-chief. But regardless of what the Rump might order, Monck's troops remained loyal to him, and with public opinion with Monck, the Rump realised that the writing was on the wall, and a free Parliament was called. Londoners reacted to the news enthusiastically, buying Monck's soldiers drinks and inviting them to share rumps of roasted beef. Thus the so called 'Long Parliament' dissolved itself and just as an unholy alliance of Scottish Presbyterians and Royalists had supported Charles II in 1650–51, it was the return of the Presbyterians and Royalist sympathisers to the 'Convention Parliament' in 1660 which paved the way for the Restoration of Charles II nine years later.

But it was not until April that Monck formally pledged himself to the return of the King. Following the receipt of the Declaration of Breda, Charles II's manifesto for the Restoration of the Monarchy, Monck committed himself and the army to a peaceful Restoration. The news of the Declaration was greeted by Londoners drinking the King's health on their knees, and as Pepys noted, everyone had become a Royalist. As for Monck, until the King stepped back on British soil, he was the most powerful man in the country. On 1 May, Charles was formally invited to return as King, and on 25 May, he landed at Dover. On 29 May, Charles journeyed to Blackheath where Monck had assembled his army for review. From there, Charles went to Deptford where he was welcomed by the Lord Mayor and Aldermen before finally moving, in procession, to Whitehall. At two o'clock in the afternoon of Tuesday, 29 May 1660, on his 30th birthday, Charles II entered the capital which he had last seen as a boy of 10. The Monarchy was restored.

---

3   Urban, *Generals*, p. 17.

The Gazetteer of Civil War London

There are nearly 200 sites across London associated with the capital's military role during the 1640s and 1650s. A significant number of these are still visible or at least traceable, whilst others are remembered by modern streets of the occasional memorial. The following pages list these sites alphabetically, setting them out in two groups: inside the Lines of Communication, and outside the Lines of Communication. The use of italics indicates that a site is no longer in existence. The grid reference is as close to the centre of the site as possible, or, in the case of roads, at its middle. Where the site is a district, than the grid reference is that of a notable building that existed during the period, more often than not, the local parish church.[1]

Inside the Lines of Communication

Adams Court (TQ 3287 8133)
Thomas Adams (1586–1668) lived here in the 1640s when he was Master of the Draper's Company. Lord Mayor in 1645, he was subsequently arrested for his Royalist sympathies. Adams Court is named after him.

Aldersgate Street (TQ 3203 8156)
In 1644, Thanet House (later known as Shaftesbury House) was built for the Earl of Thanet by Inigo Jones. During the Civil War, another house, Petre House, was used as a prison, and the Royalist poet, Richard Lovelace, was kept there in 1648. Writing in 1657, Howell said 'Aldersgate resembleth an Italian street more than any other in London by reason of the spaciousness and uniformity of buildings, and the straightness thereof, with the convenient distance of the houses; on both sides where of there are divers fair ones'.

---

1   The grid references have been identified using Free Map Tools (<https://www.freemaptools.com/>).

THE GAZETTEER OF CIVIL WAR LONDON

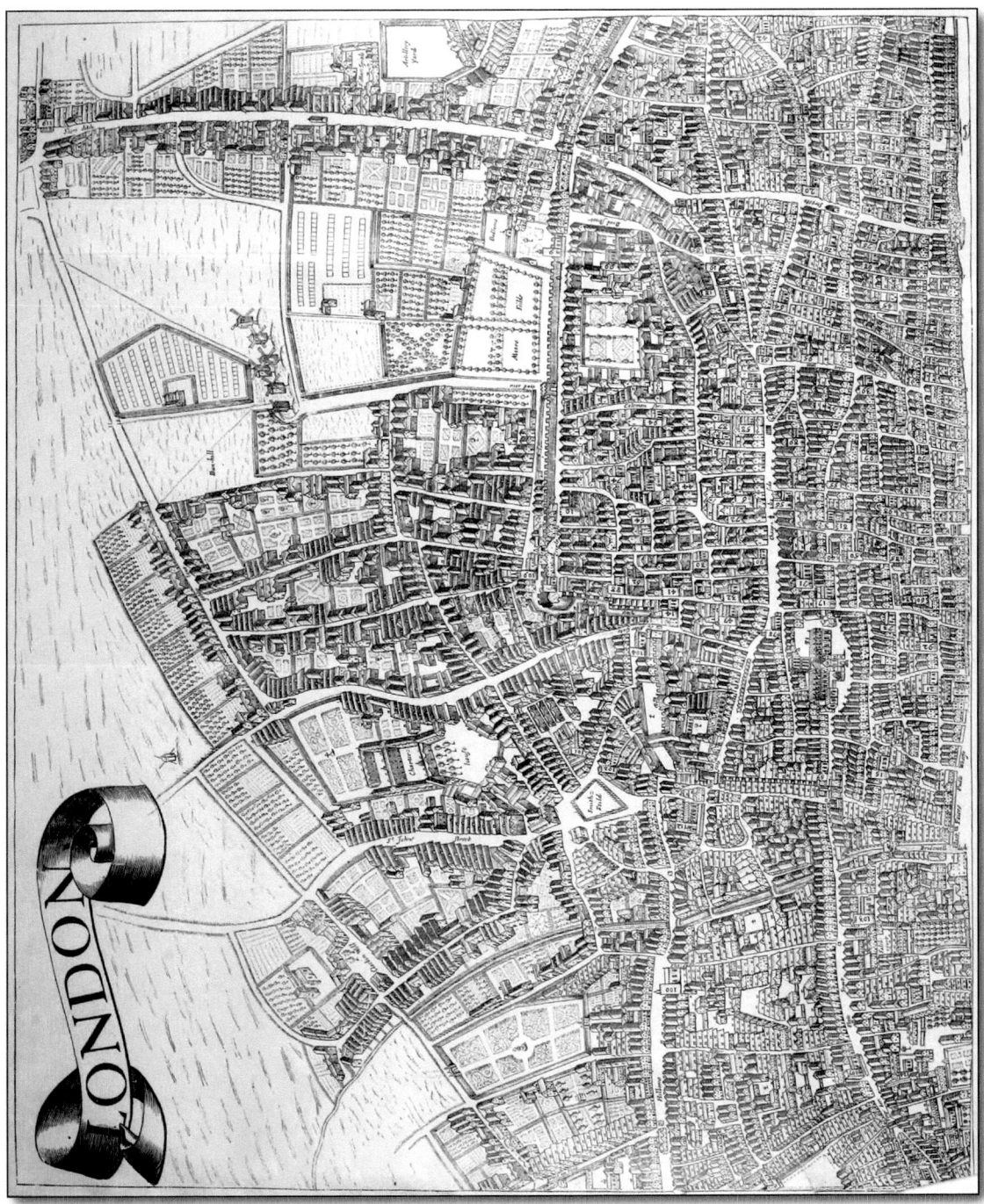

Faithorne's 1658 map of the City of London. St Paul's Cathedral is positioned lower centre of the map. Bun-hill and Clerken Well are clearly marked, whilst the river Fleet runs north to south to the west of St Pauls. Other churches featured include St Katharine Cree (43) and St Stephen Coleman (94).

CIVIL WAR LONDON

Norden's 1593 map of Westminster. Whilst dating 50 years prior to the Civil Wars, a number of the great houses which lined the Strand can be clearly identified. Also visible are Charinge Crosse and the Convent Garden.

All Hallows Barking (by the Tower), Byward Street (TQ 3326 8074)
Many of those executed on Tower Hill are buried here, including Archbishop William Laud (until he was reburied in St John's, Oxford, in 1663). On 4 January 1650, 27 barrels of gunpowder exploded beside the churchyard, blowing up over 50 houses including the Rose Tavern where the parish dinner was being held, and causing many deaths. In 1658–59 the tower was rebuilt, making it the only London church to have building work carried out during the Commonwealth.

Artillery Lane (TQ 3331 8175)
'Artyllerye Lane' (recorded in 1600) takes its name from the Tasel Close Artillery Yard.

Arundel House, Arundel Street (TQ 3085 8096)
Owned by Thomas Howard, Earl of Arundel, from 1607. Wenceslaus Hollar, who enjoyed Arundel's patronage, had an apartment in Arundel House and from the roof drew his view of London which was published in 1647, a year after Arundel had died. Arundel House was used as a garrison for Parliamentarian troops and during the Commonwealth distinguished visitors were received there. After the Restoration it was returned to Thomas's grandson, Henry, 6th Duke of Norfolk. The site of Arundel House (demolished in 1678) is marked by Arundel Street.

'The Anchor', Bankside (TQ 3233 8048)
The Anchor is the last of the riverside inns that existed in Shakespeare's time. It probably owes its name to an early owner of the brewery, Josiah Child, who during the 1650s was a victualler to the Commonwealth navy, supplying it with 'Masts, Spars and Bowsprits as well as stores and small beer'. Child became an MP in 1659, and the pub was known as the Anchor from around 1665. Samuel Pepys viewed the Great Fire of London from the Anchor, but the pub itself fell victim to a later fire and was rebuilt between 1770 and 1775. It is this 18th century pub which stands today.

Banqueting House, Whitehall (TQ 3005 8007)
The only remaining part of the old Palace of Whitehall, the Banqueting House was designed by Inigo Jones and completed in 1622. It was used for a variety of state and court ceremonies, but it is as the place of the execution of Charles I that it is best known. On 30 January 1649, the King walked for the last time across the Banqueting House, and out through a window onto the scaffold which had been erected against the wall of a now demolished brick extension to the north of the main building. He made a brief speech, declaring himself 'the Martyr of the People' before he was beheaded.

Bartholomew Close (TQ 3185 8174)
Named after the nearby church of St Bartholomew the Great, in 1633 Hubert Le Sueur lived here while making the equestrian statue of Charles I. During the spring of 1660, John Milton hid in the Close until the Act of Oblivion pardoned him.

Above: Bunhill Fields Burial Ground: established in 1665 and the place of burial of General Charles Fleetwood. (David Flintham)

Below: The tomb of John Bunyan in Bunhill Fields Burial Ground. (David Flintham)

Berkeley Square (TQ 2865 8063)
Soon after the Restoration, Lord Berkeley of Stratton, former Royalist commander in Devon and governor of Exeter, acquired extensive lands to the north of Piccadilly and it is after him that Berkeley Square is named.

Bridewell (TQ 3150 8098)
In 1556 the City of London took possession of Bridewell Palace, turning it into a prison. It was used as a prison for Royalist prisoners, and later Parliamentarian troops billeted themselves at Bridewell, refusing to leave until they received their pay.

Bruton Street (TQ 2873 8075)
Extending from Berkeley Square to New Bond Street, Bruton Street is named after Bruton in Somerset, which was close to the country estate of Lord Berkeley.

Buckingham Street (TQ 3021 8053)
From 1687, 12 Buckingham Street was the town house of Mary, Lady Falconburg, Cromwell's daughter.

Bunhill Fields, City Road (TQ 3260 8229)
Taking its name from Bone Hill (and linked either to Smithfield Market or the charnel house in St Paul's Churchyard), the graveyard of Bunhill Fields was established in 1665–56. Never consecrated, it became a popular place of burial for nonconformists; indeed, it has been said that Bunhill Fields is the graveyard of the English Revolution as within its walls are the graves of Puritan leaders, soldiers, statesmen and writers and members of Cromwell's own family (two tombs bear the Cromwell name – 'R Cromwell' and 'H Cromwell'). Other notable graves include:

- John Bunyan (1628–1688), author of *Pilgrim's Progress* (the most translated book after the Bible)
- Lieutenant General Charles Fleetwood (d. 1692). Married the eldest daughter of Oliver Cromwell (following the death of Henry Ireton), was Lord Deputy of Ireland (1654–1657), the chief mourner at Cromwell's funeral, and temporarily commander-in-chief of the army in 1660.

Bunhill Row (TQ 3250 8222)
Named after Bunhill Fields, John Milton lived here from 1662 to his death in 1674.

Canon Row (TQ3021 7976)
Named after the canons of St Stephen's Chapel, Canon Row was the location of Derby House, a Tudor mansion demolished in the 18th century. The house was used by the Committee of Both Kingdoms, Parliament's principle executive committee (which was also known as the Derby House Committee). John Pym died here in 1643.

CIVIL WAR LONDON

Hollar's etching of the equestrian statue of King Charles I, on the site of the original Charing Cross, the place of execution of several regicides. (Thomas Fisher Rare Book Library, University of Toronto)

Charing Cross (TQ 2992 8042)

Charing Cross was one of 12 Eleanor Crosses built by Edward I to mark the stopping points of his queen's body prior to its burial in Westminster Abbey in 1290. It was pulled down by 'furious and zealous Parliamentarians' (John Evelyn's words) in 1647, but the site was where eight regicides were executed. On 13 October 1660, Pepys went 'to Charing-cross to see Major-Generall Harrison [who had been condemned 2 days before] hanged, drawn, and quartered – which was done there – he looking as cheerfully as any man could in that condition. He was presently cut down and his head and his heart shown to the people, at which there was great shouts of joy'. Pepys continues, 'Thus it was my chance to see the King beheaded at Whitehall and to see the first blood shed in revenge for the blood of the King at Charing-cross'. Harrison was followed by John Carew (15 October), John Cooke and Hugh Peters (16 October), and John James, Adrian Scroope, Thomas Scot and Gregory Clement (17 October). Such was the stench from the burnings, that further executions were moved to Tyburn. Hubert le Sueur's 1632–33 equestrian statue of Charles I now stands on the site (it was erected there in 1674–75 on a plinth designed by Wren). A Victorian replica of the cross now stands in the forecourt of Charing Cross railway station.

Cheapside Cross (TQ 3218 8125)

At Westcheap (now Cheapside) Cross was another of the Eleanor Crosses. The 17th century cross was the third incarnation of the monument, which had been reconstructed and refurbished several times before 1642. Whilst previously enjoying the protection of the mayor and Corporation of London, in the years running up to the English Civil War the cross encompassed the doctrinal debates of the period. The Puritans identified the cross with 'Dagon', the ancient god of the Philistines, viewing it as the embodiment of Catholic tradition. In 1642, the Parliamentarians formed the Committee for the Demolition of Monuments of Superstition and Idolatry, led by Sir Robert Harley and the destruction of the cross was a priority. At least one riot was fought in its shadow as opponents of the cross descended upon it to pull it down and supporters rallied to stop them. The cross was finally demolished in May 1643 (fragments are displayed in the Museum of London). Though less well known than the Charing Cross, the downfall of the Cheapside Cross is one of the most important examples of iconoclasm in English history.

Christ Church Greyfriars, Newgate Street (TQ 3188 8144)

A former Franciscan church which became a parish church at the Dissolution, on 7 June 1649 MPs and senior army officers, including Cromwell, Fairfax, and Ireton, attending a service of thanksgiving here for the apparent end of the wars. Kenelm Digby was buried in the church in 1665. Damaged in the Great Fire, it was destroyed in the Blitz and now only the tower survives.

Clerkenwell Manor, **Ashby Street** (TQ 3170 8273)
On the corner of Ashby Street, which leads from St John's Street Road to Northampton Square, is the site of the old manor house of Clerkenwell, the residence of the Compton family until nearly the end of the 17th century. Spencer Compton, 2nd Earl of Northampton, fought for the King at Edgehill and was killed, famously refusing quarter, at the Battle of Hopton Heath on 19 March 1643. His three sons accompanied him at Hopton Health and his eldest son, James, succeeded as the 3rd Earl of Northampton. He was equally active for the King's cause, fighting at the First Battle of Newbury, Cropredy Bridge, Lostwithiel, and during the Newbury campaign in October 1644. He relieved Banbury Castle (26 October 1644). Defeated by Cromwell at Islip (23 April 1645), he commanded the second line of the Royalist Horse on the right flank of the army at the defeat at Naseby. Of the 2nd Earl's other sons, Henry Compton became bishop of London and Sir William Compton, according to Cromwell 'the sober young man, and the godly cavalier', was captured and subsequently released following the siege of Colchester in 1648, and was later one of the original members of the secret Royalist organisation, *The Sealed Knot*. The 3rd Earl returned to Clerkenwell after the Restoration, his estates, which had been confiscated by Parliament, having been returned.

Coleman Street (TQ 3252 81477
Coleman Street was London's radical heart: the parish of St Stephen's, Coleman Street, had a reputation for disorder dating back to the beginning of the 17th century. Isaac Penington had a house on Coleman Street, and it was to here that the five members fled in in January 1642. In Coleman Street stood the *Star Inn* (long since demolished), a favourite meeting place for leading Parliamentarians, and it was likely that it was here, towards the end of 1648, that Cromwell plotted the trial and execution of the King.

Copt Hall (TQ 3026 7839)
Situated on the river in what is now Vauxhall, a facility for the development of artillery set up in 1629. It produced light artillery pieces for the man Parliamentarian armies during the early years of the Civil War, although production probably continued until the end of the decade. It was later home to artists and inventors, coming into the possession of first the Marquis of Worcester, and, after the Restoration, Sir Samuel Morland.

Covent Garden (TQ 3025 8095)
In 1630 the Duke of Bedford commissioned Inigo Jones to develop his land at 'Convent Garden and the Long Acre', into a square in the Palladio style. The area became quickly known as 'Covent Garden'; its two-storey houses appealed to people of quality, who flocked to St Paul's church on the west of the piazza. But it soon became London's premier flesh market as the brothels moved here from Clerkenwell and Moorfields.

Downing Street (TQ 2991 7990)
Elizabeth I leased the former brewhouse known as the Axe to Thomas Knyvet, keeper of Whitehall Palace in 1581. After the death of his widow, the property was passed to his niece, Elizabeth Hampden, mother of John and aunt of Oliver Cromwell. Soon afterwards, the Crown's interest in the property was acquired by Sir George Downing who, in around 1680, built a cul-de-sac of plain brick terraced houses. Downing Street now covers the location of Hampden House, the London residence of John Hampden (k. 1643).

Drapers Hall, Throgmorton Street (TQ 3278 8136)
In April 1660 it was used by General Monck as a headquarters. Destroyed in the Great Fire, it was rebuilt in 1667, and again in the 19th century.

Drury Lane (TQ 3030 8123)
A fashionable residential street during the 17th century. Residents included the Marquis of Argyll and the Earl of Stirling in 1634–37, and Oliver Cromwell in 1646.

Durham House, Durham House Street, Strand (TQ 3021 8066)
A town house for the Bishops of Durham, during the 17th century, ambassadors were lodge here. In 1640, the Bishop sold his interest to the Earl of Pembroke, but his plans for rebuilding were halted by the Civil War. During the war, Parliamentary troops were quartered here. The site of the mansion is commemorated by Durham House Street.

Ely House, Ely Place (TQ 3132 8171)
Between 1643 and 1648, Ely House, part of the Bishops of Ely's London residence, was a prison for Royalist prisoners of war, but in 1648 it was converted into a military hospital. The large hall, chapel and cloistered quadrangle were utilised in the hospital complex, while to the south, there were large gardens including a herb garden. Lady Hatton (widow of Sir Christopher Hatton who leased the house from the Bishops) died in 1648 and in 1660 the Bishops of Ely returned.

Essex House, Essex Street, Strand (TQ 3093 8103)
Once the Outer Temple of the Knights Templar, the house was inherited by Robert Devereux, Earl of Essex in 1588. When his son, Robert, came of age, he lived there and did so until his death in 1646. Commander of the Parliamentarian army at the outbreak of the Civil War, in 1643 the House of Commons led by the Speaker, the Lord Mayor and the Aldermen came to congratulate him after the First Battle of Newbury. When Essex died, his body lay in state here (witnessed by the 13-year-old Samuel Pepys). In 1674, the estate was sold to Nicholas Barbon and soon demolished. The site is now marked by Essex Street and Devereux Court.

Fetter Lane (TQ 3118 8156)
Public executions were carried out at either end of Fetter Lane. Nathaniel Tomkins, brother-in-law of Edmund Waller, was executed at the Holborn end,

before his front door, on 5 July 1643 for his part in the Royalist conspiracy known as Waller's Plot.

Finsbury (TQ 3274 8204)
From the time of the Civil War until after the Restoration there was a foundry in Finsbury Fields where cannon were made. In May 1642, the City Regiments of the London Trained Bands were reviewed on Finsbury Fields.

Fleet Prison (TQ 3151 8135)
From the reign of Henry VIII until 1641, prisoners convicted by the Court of Star Chamber were imprisoned in the Fleet Prison which stood on the east bank of the Fleet River. The physician George Thomson (*c*.1619–1676) was imprisoned for a time here following his capture by parliamentary forces at Newbury in 1644.

Fortune Playhouse, **Golden Lane** (TQ 3224 8216)
Modelled on the Globe in Southwark, the Fortune playhouse was similar in size and design to the Red Bull theatre and like the Red Bull was home to old-fashioned plays performed for noisy, ignorant audiences and in later years it was the cause of, or scene of, numerous brawls violent enough to result in court cases. The wooden original burnt down in 1621 but was rebuilt in brick. Closed by order of Parliament in 1642, illegal performances continued, and during the 1650s soldiers defaced the Fortune, and actors were arrested for performing there in 1659.

Friday Street, *Saracen's Head* (TQ 3211 8100)
The Levellers' principle constitutional manifesto, the 'Agreement of the People', was orchestrated from the *Saracen's Head* which once stood on the west side of Friday Street.

Gatehouse Prison, **Broad Sanctuary, Westminster** (TQ 2991 7964)
Built in 1370, in 1642 the Cavalier poet Richard Lovelace was incarcerated and it was whilst here he wrote his most famous poem, *To Althea* – 'Stone walls do not a prison make, nor iron bars a cage'.

Globe Theatre (TQ 3219 8044)
Burnt down in 1613 and rebuilt in 1614, the *Globe* fell into disuse around 1642 when performances were banned. It was closed down in 1644 and demolished three years later.

Goldsmiths Hall, **Foster Lane** (TQ 3210 8141)
The original Goldsmiths Hall (the current building dates from 1829–35), built around 1366, was used as the exchequer, 1641–60. This building was damaged in the Great Fire and restored in 1669.

Great Ormond Street (TQ 3042 8209)
Great Ormond Street was probably named after James Butler, first Duke of Ormond who was the Royalist commander in Ireland.

Great Scotland Yard (TQ 3006 8034)
Inigo Jones is said to have lived here for a while whilst he was Surveyor General, and during the Commonwealth he and the sculptor Nicholas Stone buried their money in the garden for safekeeping (they later moved it to Lambeth Marsh). John Milton had lodgings here whilst he was Cromwell's Latin Secretary.

Grocers' Hall, Princes Street (TQ 3250 8126)
In January 1642, committees of both Houses of Parliament met here to discuss Charles' botched attempt to arrest the Five Members. Requisitioned by Parliament at the outbreak of the war, it was used by various Parliamentary and non-Parliamentary committees during the 1640s and 1650s. On 7 June 1649 both Cromwell and Fairfax were entertained here: 'The musick was only drums and trumpets, the feast very sumptuous, no healths drunk nor any incivility passed'. Cromwell was presented with £300 of gold plate and 200 pieces of gold, whilst Fairfax received a basin and ewer in beaten gold. In 1654 the division of Ireland was determined here, and at the Restoration, the company held a feast in celebration and made Charles II the Sovereign Master. The current hall is the fourth on the site; the first was badly damaged during the Great Fire and was completely rebuilt in 1668–89.

Guildhall (TQ 3237 8142)
The great hall, built between 1411 and 1440, probably stands on the site of an earlier Saxon guildhall. It is the only non-ecclesiastical stone building in the City to have survived to the present day, despite having been damaged in both the Great Fire and the Blitz. On 12 December 1642, it was the scene of considerable unrest when peace petitioners, hoping to bring about an end to the war, were attacked by those in favour of the war. The peace protestors barricaded themselves inside the Guildhall whilst their opponents, joined by some Parliamentarian troops (who even brought up two cannon) attempted to force entry. Allowed to leave by the Court of Common Council, once outside, the peace protestors were pursued at sword point, one having to flee to the roof of a house, escaping by 'leaping from one house top to another.'

Gun Street (TQ 3339 8177)
Gun Street takes its name from the artillery yard that stood nearby in Tudor times, 'whereunto,' according to Stow, 'the gunners of the Tower do weekly repair'.

Gunpowder Alley, Shoe Lane (TQ 3133 8136)
During the 17th century, Shoe Lane was known for its signwriters and broadsheets. Home to John de Critz, serjeant painter to Charles I, in 1651 the mapmaker John Ogilby (1600–1676) also lived here. In 1657, in a mean lodging in Gunpowder Alley (between Shoe Lane and Fetter Lane), the poet Richard Lovelace died.

Hatton House, Saffron Hill (TQ 3133 8193)
On lands originally part of the Bishopric of Ely, Hatton House was used as a prison in 1642. During the second half of the 17th century, the majority of the Bishop's Palace estate was demolished.

Haydon Square, **Minories (TQ 3343 8085)**
Named after Captain John Heydon (or Haydon) who was Lieutenant General of the Ordnance during the reign of Charles I. Heydon was resident in the nearby Minories.

Henrietta Street (TQ 3019 8086)
Built between 1631 and 1634, it was named after Queen Henrietta Maria. On Henrietta Street was the studio of Samuel Cooper who famously was commanded to paint a portrait of Oliver Cromwell 'warts and all'.

Horse Guards, Whitehall (TQ 2996 8014)
On the Tiltyard of Whitehall Palace, in 1649 a small guardhouse was built only to be replaced by larger accommodation for the horse guards and some of the foot guards in 1663–65. The two on the clock on the current building is marked in black which commemorates the execution of Charles I which took place at two o'clock on the afternoon of 30 January 1649 outside the Banqueting House (opposite).

Hyde Park (TQ 2768 8034)
Opened to the public from early in the 17th century, Hyde Park was the site of one of the forts and connecting ramparts (traces of which can still be seen today) which were built in 1642–43, and was also used for military camps. In 1652, the park was sold by order of Parliament, but the following year, as John Evelyn noted, 'the sordid fellow' who had purchased part of the park, was charging 1s for every coach and 6d for every horse to enter it. May Day 1654 'was more observed by people going a-maying than for divers years past. Great resort came to Hyde Park, many hundreds of rich coaches and gallants in attire but most shameful powdered hair, men painted and spotted women.' Also popular at the time were coach races, and on one occasion Cromwell himself 'provoked the horses [so much] with the whip that they grew unruly and ran so fast that the postilion could not hold them in whereby His Highness [Cromwell] was flung out of the coachbox upon the pole, on which he lay with his body and afterwards fell upon the ground. His foot getting hold of the tackling, he was carried away a good while in that posture during which time a pistol went off in his pocket. But at last he got his foot clear and so came to escape.' At the Restoration, the park returned to the Crown.

King Street **(TQ 3013 8089)**
The main route from Westminster Abbey to Charing Cross, running down the western fringe of Whitehall Palace, named after Charles I, the street was laid out by Inigo Jones in 1637. A statue of Charles I by Le Sueur stood here until the end of the Civil War when it was taken down. Cromwell had a house here in 1648, probably on the east side of King Street, near its northern end. Those who lived in the street included William Lenthall, Speaker of the House of Commons during the Commonwealth, Thomas Killigrew, the dramatist (1637–43), and Sir Kenelm Digby, the writer and diplomat (1662–85). The house that Digby lived in would later become the first family

CIVIL WAR LONDON

Memorial to John Thurloe, Secretary of State, in Chancery Lane. (David Flintham)

hotel in London. The present St Margret Street, Parliament Street and Whitehall approximately follow its course.

Lambeth Bridge (TQ 3037 7906)
Before the bridge was built, this was the site of a horse ferry. When Archbishop Laud was moving into Lambeth Palace in 1633, the ferry sank under the weight of his belongings. In 1656, Oliver Cromwell's coach and horses also sank whilst crossing here.

Lambeth Palace (TQ 3048 7910)
Probably dating from the 13th century (although added to since then, including the Tudor gatehouse in 1486–1501), Lambeth Palace is the London residence of the Archbishop of Canterbury. During the 1630s Archbishop Laud undertook much restoration work including renewing the altar and putting in a carved screen (now in the Lollards' Tower, which itself dates from 1434–35). His restoration work was brought against him at his trial. On 11 May 1640 Laud was attacked here by 500 London apprentices and was forced to flee to Whitehall, noting in his diary 'I had notice and strengthened the house as well as I could and, God be blessed I had no harm.' The following month, John Evelyn records another attack by 'a rude rabble from Southwark.' During the Civil War the Palace was used as a prison, inmates including the poet Richard Lovelace in 1648–49. The chapel was used for dances during the Commonwealth, whilst the corpse of Archbishop Parker (1504–1575) was dug up and reburied under a dung hill.

Lincoln's Inn Chapel (TQ 3081 8146)
The chapel was built between 1619–23, probably to the designs of Inigo Jones. Within the chapel are the remains of John Thurloe, Cromwell's Secretary of State, who had chambers in the Inn from 1646 until his death in 1668. Also buried here is the pamphleteer William Prynne, who died in 1669. Importantly, it was in the undercroft that in 1659 that 80 members of Parliament met in what was the first move towards the Restoration.

THE GAZETTEER OF CIVIL WAR LONDON

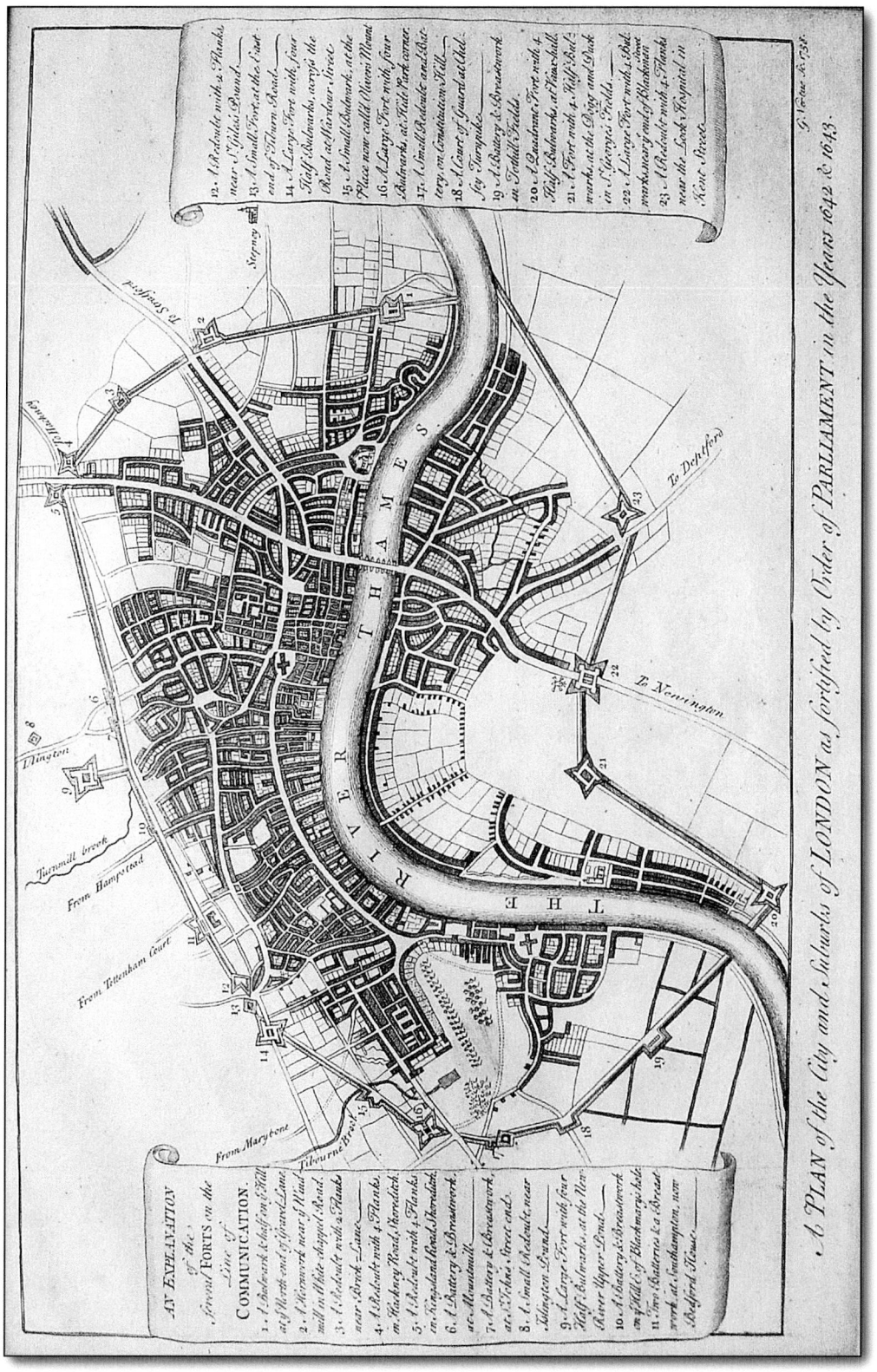

George Vertue's plan of London's Civil War defences, drawn a century after the defences were actually built. (David Flintham)

Lincoln's Inn Fields (TQ 3051 8143)

First recorded as Lincolnes Inne Feildes in 1598, the fields were laid out and surrounded by town houses to a design by Inigo Jones from 1618 onwards. However, work did not actually commence until the 1630s when William Newton of Beddenham in Bedfordshire was finally granted permission to build 32 houses. Lindsey House (No 59/60), completed around 1638–40, has been attributed to Inigo Jones, although the builder may have been David Cunningham. This is the oldest house on the square and survives to this day. The majority of the houses had been completed by 1641. Whilst it was a fashionable place to live, the grassland in the centre of the square often witnessed fights and robberies and was a place of execution until the 1680s (in 1683, William, Lord Russell, was executed here for his role in the Rye House Plot).

Lincoln's Inn Gatehouse (TQ 3091 8154)

Built in 1517–21 by Sir Thomas Lovell (and reconstructed in 1966–69), the rooms above the gate are said to have been occupied in 1617 by Oliver Cromwell, then an 18-year-old law student. Cromwell's son, Richard (Lord Protector, 1658–59) also studied here. Between 1646 and 1659, John Thurloe occupied a chamber in the south side of the Gatehouse, and his association with the area is commemorated by a Cromwell Association plaque in Chancery Lane.

The Lines of Communication

The construction of its fortifications in 1642–43 deserves to be recognised as one of London's greatest achievements of the entire Civil War period. London's defences were developed in two phases. The first, in 1642, took the form of blocking streets with barriers or chains (one location was Smithfield Barrs, at the bottom of St John Street – TQ 316 818), the building of guardhouses and some small redoubts guarding main roads. This was initially a hurried reaction to the threat of a Royalist advance from the Midlands in the autumn of 1642, and recognition that the existing city walls protected just a small area of London. And whilst London had grown far beyond the City walls, there is archaeological evidence for the reuse of the existing medieval defences. However, construction was apparently sufficiently advanced by December 1642 to attract the attention of diarist John Evelyn who, on 7 December 1642, 'went from Wotton to Lond[on], to see the so much celebrated line of communication.' Recent studies suggest that the defences, at least in the north-western sector, were sufficiently strong enough to be considered the anvil against which the hammers of two Parliamentarian armies could crush the Royalists in late autumn 1642.

In February 1643, the defences were surveyed and proposals for a circuit of forts were presented to the Court of Common Council by Colonel (Alderman) Randall Mainwaring. Mainwaring was a colonel in Warwick's army, a lieutenant colonel in the Red Regiment of the Trained Bands, deputy Lord Mayor to Isaac Penington and later succeeded Philip Skippon as Sargeant Major General of the City. These proposals were formalised into a resolution of common council which, together with a recommendation to form a Committee of Fortifications to coordinate construction were approved by the Common Council and were subsequently ratified by Parliament on 7 March 1643.

Whilst Mainwaring outlined the location and specification of the forts, he did not actually design them. Some studies have suggested that Skippon designed the defences as he had experience of siege warfare, haven been present at the sieges of Breda and Maastricht. Alternatively, the Venetian Ambassador, Gerolamo Agostini hinted that they may have been of Dutch design – he noted on 13 March 1643 that 'they have sent to Holland for engineers'. It was the Dutch school of military engineering that was the most readily applied, and the dominant characteristics of Dutch fortifications, namely the earth rampart and ditch, suited London's circumstances and topography.

By the end of March, work was well underway, entailing a massive amount of unpaid labour. Volunteers came from all walks of London life, including the Livery Companies, the Trained Bands and the Court of Common Council. At any one time, as many as 20,000, men, women and children (possibly including a nine-year old Samuel Pepys), would be labouring on the fortifications, a fact that was not left unnoticed by the Royalists who mocked their labours. In his *Hudibras*, Samuel Butler satirises the women who:

> March'd rank and file with drum and ensign,
> T'entrench the city for defence in.
> Rais'd rampiers with their own soft hands,
> To put the enemy to stands;
> From ladies down to oyster-wenches
> Labour'd like pioneers in trenches,
> Fell to their pick-axes and tools,
> And help'd the men dig like moles.

During April William Lithgow, a Scottish merchant and traveller, walked the entire 18 km (approx. 11 mile) circuit of forts and connecting earthworks, known as the 'Line of Communication' (yet unfinished, as it was not until mid-May that Agostini reported that the forts were complete) in a single day. Lithgow described the defences as 'erected of turffe, sand, watles, and earthen work'[2] (and masonry was used in the construction of the gateways). In his account, he says the 'trench dyke was three yards thick and on the trench side twice as high'. The defensive ditch was about 5.5 m (18 ft) wide (as much as 9 m (9½ ft) wide in one location[3]) and 1.4 m (4½ ft) deep. The defensive ditches were probably dry although there is evidence for the ditches nearer the Thames being wet.

---

2   LITHGOW, WILLIAM, *The Present Surveigh At London*, reprinted in ROSS, LIEUTENANT-COLONEL W. G., R.E., *Military Engineering during the Great Civil War, 1642–9* (London, 1984), Appendix A, pp. 82–83.

3   R. Haslam and V. Ridgeway, *Excavations at the British Museum: An Archaeological and Social History of Bloomsbury, British Museum Research Publication 210* (London: British Museum Press, 2017).

CIVIL WAR LONDON

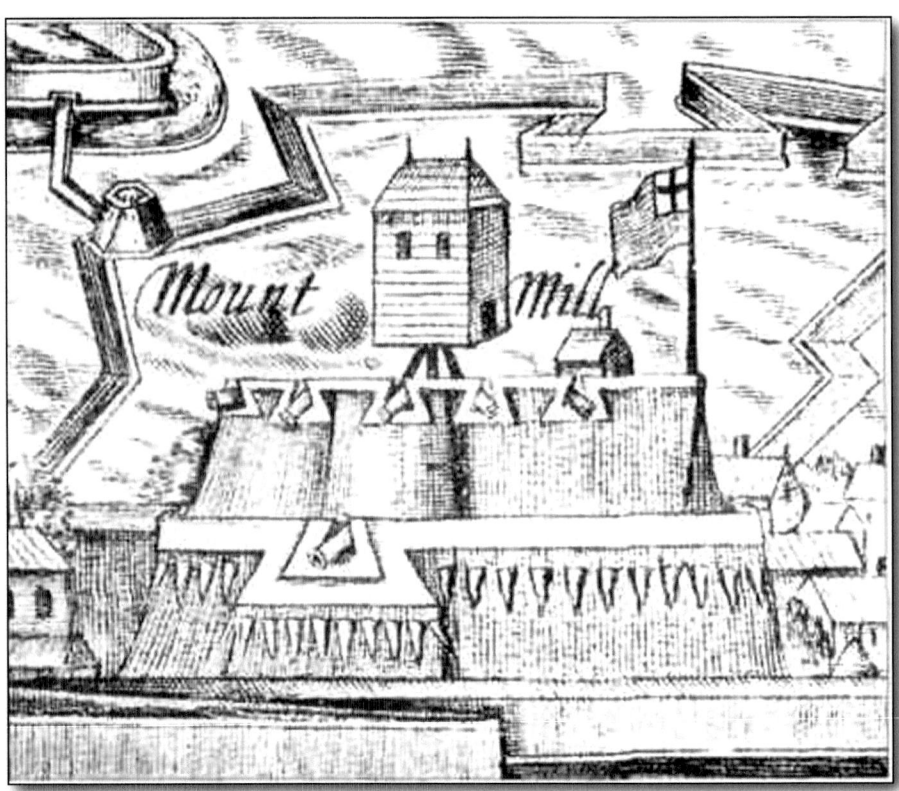

A contemporary woodcut of Mount Mill Fort, *c*.1643. (David Flintham)

Whitechapel fort was one of the first forts Lithgow encountered during his trek. Today, East Mount Street and Mount Terrace mark the site of the fort, later known as Whitechapel Mount TQ 3444 8173). After the war, debris was added to it so ultimately it stood higher than the London Hospital when it opened in 1757. The site was cleared away in the early 19th century.

Mount Mill Fort by Goswell Road (TQ 3185 8259) was a typical fort. Lithgow:

> Marched through Fineberry fields along the trench (enclosing these moorefields), and came to Mount Mil-hill Fort (for all the forts about are [......] and [......] in sight of other), where being arrived, I found it standing on the highway near to the Red Bull. This is a large and singular fortification, having a fort above, and within a fort, the lowest consisting of five angles, two whereof towards the fields are each of them thrice ported, having as many great cannon, with a flanking piece from a hid corner; the upper fort standing circular, is furnished with eleven pieces of cannon reall [Royal], which command all the rest; and upon the bosome top of all standeth a windmill; the lower bulwarks are first pallosaded round about and near their tops, and then in the middle flank between the two ditches strongly barricaded; besides tow counterscarps and three redoubts of lesser importance, yet all defensive. This is one of the chief forts about the city and first erected.

In 1644, Hollar sketched Hyde Park Fort and this is the most accurate representation of any part of the defences. The year before, however, Hollar had been at Oxford with the Royalist army. One is left to wonder, then, if

Wenceslaus Hollar's 1644 sketches of Hyde Park Fort – drawn from a position in what is today Piccadilly. (Copyright of The University of Manchester)

The only remains of the fortifications constructed in 1642–43 is this stretch of ramparts in Hyde Park, running parallel to Park Lane. (David Flintham)

Hollar's 1644 visit was entirely innocent or, like Kenelm Digby the year before, he was spying for the King. Hyde Park itself contains the only traces of the defences still visible today (TQ 2815 8029).

It is impossible to say how the defences would have stood up to attack as the Royalists never again approached London. But was defence the only purpose of the defences? Agostini certainly did not think so, as 'The shape they take betrays that they are not only for the defence against the royal armies, but also against tumults of the citizens, and to ensure a prompt obedience on all occasions'.

Demolition of the defences followed very closely the end of the Civil War and the Army's occupation of London in 1647. But despite the demolition work, traces of many of the forts could still be seen for years after and features remained long enough for them to be included in 18th century maps. Rocque's map shows, for instance, the *Dog and Duck* tavern (so called because it was situated close to ponds where spaniels hunted duck), which is surrounded by traces of St Georges Fields Fort (TQ 3123 7927).

The site of Fort Royal on today's Pentonville Road (TQ 3106 8312) in particular has been drawn, mapped and described on several occasions – one of a series of engravings by Hollar in 1665, clearly shows the remains of the (eastern?) defensive ditch and as late as 1756, enough remained for Maitland to describe them – in spite of the building of the New River Company's Upper Pond in 1708 which was constructed on the site of the eastern portion of the fort. Viewing the site of Fort Royal today, the brick-walled 1856 reservoir, strengthened by sloping earth banks is clear to see. It is only coincidence that the site of the fort is now occupied by a structure that has a passing resemblance to the original Fort Royal.

It is unlikely that the purpose of the fortifications was ever meant to be purely as a system of military defence. As previously noted, it has been

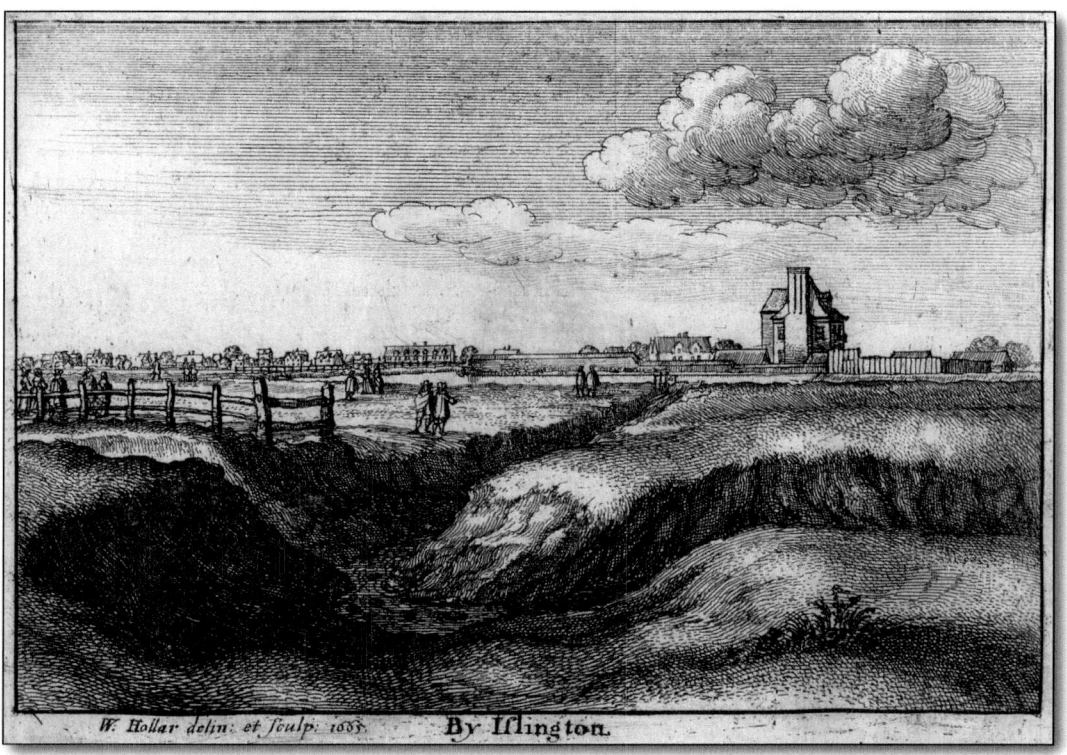

Wenceslaus Hollar's 1665 view of London from Islington. The remains of the ditch from Fort Royal can be clearly seen. (Thomas Fisher Rare Book Library, University of Toronto)

suggested elsewhere that there was a tactical use for the fortifications that were in place by autumn 1642, and as the Venetian Ambassador noted, they also existed to exercise a degree of control over Londoners, and at the same time were a way of controlling traffic in and out of London, permitting tolls to be collected. In addition, the fortifications also gave citizens confidence that London was protected, a factor that was also important to those home and abroad wanting to trade with London, thus the existence of the fortifications stated that London was secure and open for business.

London Bridge (TQ 3275 8065)
During the Civil War, cannon were set up behind the bridge gates but were never used. Built during the 12th and 13th centuries, the bridge lasted for 600 years. At the Southwark end of the bridge was the Great Stone Gate where the heads of several regicides were displayed on spikes following their execution. Close to the foot of London Bridge was a pub called The Bear-at-the-Bridge-Foot, and during the 1650s its landlord was a former New Model Army colonel, Cornelius Cooke. The bridge was to the east of the current London Bridge, following the line of the modern Fish Street Hill.

London Wall
Repaired and reinforced as part of London's defence in 1642, sections of the City wall can still be seen (travelling east to west) at the Tower of London (Wardrobe Tower); Tower Hill (TQ 3350 8080); Cooper's Row; All Hallows London Wall; London Wall (in the underground carpark); St Alfege's churchyard (just off London Wall); Wallside; Cripplegate Bastion (beside St

Giles-without-Cripplegate – TQ 3218 8173); Wall and turret foundations in the garden of the Museum of London (Noble Street – TQ 3217 8164); and Newgate Bastion in Newgate Street.

Long Acre (TQ 3017 8110)
Originally a narrow strip of market gardens owned by the monks of Westminster Abbey, by the mid-17th century it was a fashionable address. The sculptor Nicholas Stone had a house here (1615–45), John Dryden kept an inn called the Mourning Crown (1645–53), and Cromwell had a house on the street during 1637–43.

Lothbury (TQ 3259 8131)
Just a short distance from Coleman Street is Lothbury, along which were two taverns favoured by radicals. The *Windmill Tavern* was favoured by the Levellers, as was the nearby *Whalebone Tavern*. The latter had such strong Leveller associations, that Levellers were sometimes referred to as 'Whaleboners'.

Ludgate Hill (TQ 3166 8121)
Named after the Lud Gate, the south-western gate in the City wall. The original gate was rebuilt in about 1215 and again in 1586 and then repaired after being damaged in the Great Fire. Like the other City gates, it was demolished in 1760. Eastwards from the gate ran Ludgate Hill which, during the 17th century, was a fashionable shopping area. John Evelyn lived at the Hawk and Pheasant Inn on Ludgate Hill in 1658–59.

Middle Temple Hall (TQ 3105 8100)
With its origins dating back to 1320, the present building was completed in 1573. Henry Ireton, Edward Hyde and John Evelyn are all associated with the Middle Temple.

Moorgate (TQ 3259 8161)
The area takes its name from the postern gate in the City wall which led out onto the fens. Built in 1415, it was repaired in 1472 and rebuilt in 1672 – the gateway made higher so that the Trained Bands could march through the gate with their pikes upright. The gate was demolished in 1762.

Mount Street (TQ 2807 8078)
Mount Street takes its name from Mount Field where (near the north end of Carpenter Street) stood, so legend has it a small earthwork known as Oliver's Mount, said to be part of London's defences built 1642–43.

New Artillery Ground (TQ 3266 8223)
With its origins dating to the reign of Henry VIII, the Honourable Artillery

Company is amongst the oldest regiments in the British Army.[4] In 1537, the Guild of St George received a Charter of Incorporation from the King, stating that the purpose of the Guild was for 'The better increase of the Defence of this our Realm and maintenance of the Science and Feat of shooting Long Bows, Cross Bows and Hand Guns'. After their first practice ground, the Artillery Garden, Spitalfields, they became known as 'The Gentlemen of the Artillery Garden', then simply as 'The Artillery Company' (at the time, the word 'artillery' was applied to archery and other missile weapons, while guns were known as 'great artillery').

At the end of the 15th century some moorland stretching north from the medieval city walls towards what was then the village of Hoxton was set aside for the exercise of archers, an area which became known as the 'Artillery Ground'. This area was already in use for archery practice as least as far back as the 1550s and is indicated on both Frans Franken's 'Copperplate' map of 1559 and the 'Agas' map (*c*.1561–70), which shows archery being practised to the north of what is now Chiswell Street. From early in the 17th century the Court of Aldermen of the City of London appointed the chief officers and paid the professional soldiers who trained members of the Company. Thus, crucially for the events that were to follow mid-century, a political element was introduced to the Company. Since 1633 the Artillery Company has been governed, like many of the City Livery Companies by a Court of Assistants (a number of committees are appointed by the Court). The Lord Mayor and Aldermen are honorary members of the Court of Assistants.

During the lead up to the Civil War, the Artillery Company had two training grounds, the Old Artillery Yard in Spitalfields and the New Artillery Ground which met the need for a permanent home and one where the Artillery Company could build its armoury. Whilst permission to build an armoury was first sought in 1635, it was not until 1641 that it was granted. Both grounds continued to be used until 1658 (although the bulk of pre-war training tended to take place at the Old Artillery Yard) when the Artillery Company took up permanent residence at the New Artillery Ground.

Not only did the Artillery Company provide officers for the Trained Bands (and had done so at least since the Armada crisis of 1588), the company also inspired the formation of other military companies (the Military Company in Westminster, and the Martial Yard in Southwark). The company also had a strong social side, whilst membership offered its members increased standing in society. The Honourable Artillery Company also had a less conservative element, and amongst its pre-war membership were a number who would later be known for their radicalism including Henry Overton, Thomas Pride, George Joyce (who, with the rank of cornet, removed the King from Holmby House on 3 June 1647), William Shambrooke (who was later killed by a poisoned bullet at the siege of Colchester in 1648), and the regicides Owen Rowe and Robert Tichborne. Both Rowe and Tichborne lived in the parish of

---

[4] The prefix Honourable, although first used in 1685, was not officially confirmed until 1860, during the reign of Queen Victoria.

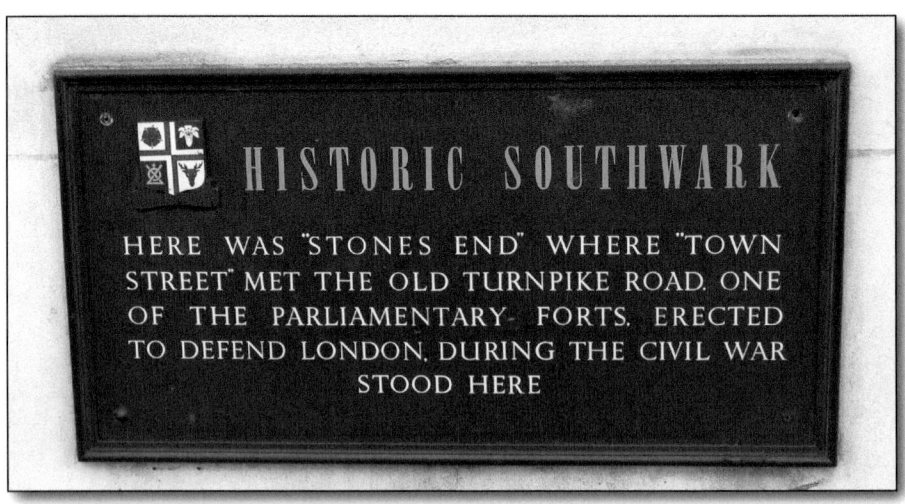

The only memorial to London's Civil War fortifications, situated on the wall of Borough Police Station. In actuality, the memorial is more than 200 metres north of the course of the defences. (David Flintham)

St Stephen's, Coleman Street, a parish where as many as a third of households were members of the HAC.

John Venn, a member of the Company since 1610, seized Windsor Castle at the outbreak of the war and continued to hold it for Parliament until June 1645. Venn, a Commissioner for the King's trial (his name and seal were on the King's death warrant), died in his sleep on 28 June 1650. But despite the very strong connection with the Trained Bands, members of the Artillery Company fought on both sides during the English Civil War: for example Robert Peake (knighted in 1645) fought for the King and was present at the fall of Basing House to Cromwell on 14 October 1645. When Peake died in 1667, he was vice-president and Leader of the Company.

The New Artillery Ground continued to be used throughout the 1640s and 50s. On 20 March 1655, some 5,000 troops were paraded prior to Phillip Skippon's appointment as the Major General for Middlesex and London. The Artillery Company participated in Cromwell's funeral procession in November 1658. The Company were ordered to attend:

> Completely armed and habited with a black feather, … the heads of the leading staffs and partizans are to be covered with cypress and the colours are to be adorned with black ribbons. Ten drums and fifes are to be provided for this occasion, the drums to be covered with black baize. [You are] not to fail in any of these premises, as you tender the honour of the City and Company.[5]

When needed within the City itself, they would enter through the Moor Gate. The actual Moor Gate was rebuilt in 1415 and survived the Great Fire. However, it was rebuilt in 1672, as Daniel Defoe in his *Tour Through the Whole Island of Great Britain*, noted:

> Moorgate is also re-built, and is a very beautiful gateway, the arch being near twenty foot high, which was done to give room for the city Trained Bands to go

---

5   Wilfrid Emberton, *Skippon's Brave Boys* (Buckingham: Quotes Limited, 1984), p. 122.

through to the Artillery Ground, where they muster, and that they might march with their pikes advanced, for then they had pikemen in every regiment, as well in the army as in the militia, which since that, is quite left off; this makes the gate look a little out of shape.

Although the Company's silver was lost during the Civil War, its archives survive from 1657 onwards (the first Annual General Court for which a record can be found was held in 1660). Latterly, Milton, Monck, Pepys and Sir Christopher Wren were all members and since the Restoration, the Company has provided Guards of Honour in the City for visits by members of the Royal Family and overseas Heads of State and are very well known for their participation in the annual Lord Mayor's Parade.

New Churchyard (Bethlem Burial Ground), Liverpool Street (TQ 328 816)
The herbalist Nicholas Culpeper (who was wounded whilst serving with the London Trained Bands at the First Battle of Newbury) was buried here in January 1654. Other burials include the Levellers Robert Lockyer (d. 1649) and John Lilburne (d. 1657).

Newcastle House, Clerkenwell Close (TQ 3137 8228)
Clerkenwell Close is the site of Newcastle House, built by the Cavendish family upon the ruins of a Benedictine nunnery. Whilst convenient for the Court, this Brick-built house was not a favourite of William Cavendish, Earl (then Marquis, and finally Duke) of Newcastle. Newcastle supported the King during the First Bishops' War (1639–40) and was later implicated in the Army Plot which forced him to leave London. In June 1642 he was appointed commander-in-chief of the Royalist counties in northern England, but went into exile following the Royalist defeat at Marston Moor in July 1644. It was whilst he was in exile in Paris that he met and married Margaret, daughter of Sir Thomas Lucas of St John's, Colchester, and sister of Sir Charles Lucas (captured at Marston Moor, and executed in 1648 following the siege of Colchester). Margaret, 31 years younger than William, was a dramatist and a writer, and is credited as being one of the first female novelists. At the Restoration Newcastle returned to London and in 1667 finally managed to buy Newcastle House back (it had been sold by Parliament in 1654). Margaret died in 1673 and the Duke himself died on Christmas Day 1676 and was buried in Westminster Abbey. Newcastle House had been demolished by 1793.

Newgate Prison (TQ 3168 8138)
A prison stood on this site in Newgate Street since the 12th century. It was rebuilt during the 17th century, and used to house Royalist prisoners. John Lilburne was imprisoned here in 1653, and in 1658 the murderer Major Strangeways was pressed to death in the Press Yard. The prison was burned down in the Great Fire and rebuilt in 1672 and was finally demolished in 1902 to make way for the Central Criminal Court.

Old Bailey (TQ 3169 8135)
First mentioned in 1585, the court originated as the sessions house of the

Lord Mayor and Sheriffs of the City of London and of Middlesex. Located next door to the older Newgate gaol (rebuilt, it would later occupy the site of Newgate itself), a number of Royalists and others were tried here during the 1640s and 50s. It was destroyed in the Great Fire of London in 1666 and rebuilt in 1674.

Petty France (TQ 293 795)
So called because French wool merchants used to live here. Its most famous resident during the 1650s was John Milton who lived in a 'pretty-garden house … opening into St James's Park'. He lived here between 1652 and 1660 when he was Latin Secretary to Oliver Cromwell. He wrote most of *Paradise Lost* here.

Pindar of Wakefield, **328 Gray's Inn Road (TQ 3043 8284)**
An Inn built in 1517 which took its name after its landlord, George Green, who had previously been Pindar (or pound-keeper) of Wakefield. The present house was built in 1878. Pindar of Wakefield was the name of the ninth fort (going anti-clockwise) of London's defences built in 1642–43, which was built nearby.

Queen's Chapel, Marlborough Gate (TQ 2928 8013)
Designed by Inigo Jones for the Infanta of Spain who was to marry the future Charles I, the Queen's Chapel was the first classical church in England. Work commenced in 1623, but was suspended when the wedding did not take place. However, it was completed for Henrietta Maria in 1626–27 and was refurnished in the 1660s for Catherine of Braganza, the Catholic Queen of Charles II.

Red Bull Theatre, **St John Street (TQ 3154 8233)**
Built in 1600 by Aaron Holland, the original open-air playhouse was renovated (and possibly roofed in) in 1625. For 60 years it entertained audiences drawn primarily from the northern suburbs, developing a reputation for rowdy, often disruptive audiences. Whilst never enjoying the fame of Southwark's theatres, it was occasionally home to companies who enjoyed Royal patronage, whilst Thomas Killigrew began his theatrical career here. Along with all the other theatres, the Red Bull was closed by the orders of Parliament in 1642. However, initially this appears to have little effect since, as late as 1648, the Red Bull was still staging performances (advertisements were thrown into gentlemen's carriages). There followed a crackdown by Parliament, which grew wiser to the real implications of advertisements for 'rope dancing' and other entertainments at the old theatres. In 1650 the Red Bull was successfully raided, a number of actors arrested and their clothes and properties confiscated, and in 1654 and again in 1655 soldiers forcibly stopped performances, but this did not prevent Sir William Davenant putting on two productions a year later . The theatre was reopened in 1660 but was destroyed during the Great Fire. After the fire, buildings were constructed on its foundations, and the outline of its structure, including the passageway from the auditorium to the street, can still be found in the street now known

as Hayward's Place off Woodbridge Street.

Red Lion Square (TQ 3050 8176)
Named after the Red Lion Inn, which was where the disinterred bodies of Cromwell, Ireton and Bradshaw lay before their desecration at Tyburn in 1661. The distance from Westminster Abbey to Tyburn is around two and a half miles, compared to nearly double this distance if the journey went via the Red Lion. Therefore, at first sight, it seems strange that following the exhumation, the three bodies, according to tradition, rested in the Red Lion (sightings of ghostly cloaked figures have been linked to this event). But the traditional final journey of the condemned commonly, starting at Newgate, proceeded along what is now Holborn, High Holborn and Oxford Street to Tyburn. This route passes close to the site of the Red Lion, and so it is possible, had they rested at the Red Lion, the bodies following the final journey of those facing execution at Tyburn. There is a theory that Cromwell's remains were in such a poor condition that his body was secretly buried in Red Lion Square and a dead solider taking his palace at Tyburn.

Salisbury Court Theatre, **Salisbury Square (TQ 3138 8114)**
Built in 1629, between 1637 and 1642, it was home to the Queen's Men theatre company. During the Commonwealth plays were illegally performed here, and in 1649 the interior was destroyed by Parliamentarian soldiers. Restored during the Restoration, it was destroyed by the Great Fire.

Salisbury House (later called Dorset House), **Fleet Street (TQ 3150 8107)**
Built on land owned by the Bishops of Salisbury, the house was purchased by Sir Richard Sackville in 1564. The Sackvilles were created Earls of Dorset in 1603, and the 4th Earl is said to have remained in the house after the execution of Charles I in 1649 until his own death in 1652. The house was destroyed in the Great Fire, and the site is now commemorated by Dorset Rise and Salisbury Square.

Savoy Palace, **Strand (TQ 3039 8073)**
The original palace (*c*.1324) was plundered and burned during the Peasants' Revolt in 1381, but the remains were only cleared way during the early 16th century when King Henry VII ordered the foundation of a hospital which was completed by 1515 and could accommodate 100 'pour and nedie' men. Engravings of the hospital show an extensive complex of buildings, including a great dormitory which was longer than Westminster Hall, and three chapels, one of which was dedicated to St John the Baptist. Parliament established a military hospital here in 1642. Described as the first of the 'modern' hospitals, there were four main wards in the church-like building: the Long Ward in the Nave, Chapel Ward in the Chancel, and the Newbury and Reading Wards in the two Transepts. Easy access to the Thames allowed casualties to be brought in by boat. In 1653, sailors wounded in the first Dutch War were admitted but they fought with the soldiers and were put under martial law. The hospital foundation was dissolved in 1702 and most of the complex was demolished in the early 19th century. All that survives today is the Chapel of St John the

Baptist, now known as The Queen's Chapel of the Savoy (TQ 30462 80787).

Smithfield (TQ 317 817)
Whilst Smithfield did not witness the number of executions in the 17th century as it did in the 16th, there was at least two executions in Smithfield during the Civil War period. In October 1644, a large crowd witnessed the hanging of Thomas Pits who had attempted to betray the Parliamentarian garrison of Rushall Hall in Staffordshire to the King, and William James 'for running away from his colours.'

Somerset House, Strand (TQ 3066 8082)
This was the site of the first Renaissance palace in England (the current building dates from the 1770s) and was built in 1547–50 for Lord Protector Somerset. The house was given to Charles I's mother, Anne of Denmark (and was renamed Denmark House) in 1603, but following her death in 1619, it was given to Charles, but he preferred St James's Palace. The house was then given to Henrietta Maria and in 1630–35 a new chapel, designed by Inigo Jones, was built (the consecration ceremonies lasted three days). During the Civil War the house was taken over by Parliament and the name reverted to Somerset House. The chapel was wrecked, and on 21 June 1652, Inigo Jones died in the house. In June 1656, Lucy Walters, one-time mistress of the future Charles II, fled the Hague with her son James, the future Duke of Monmouth. They ended up taking rooms close to Somerset House. Following his death in September 1658, Cromwell lay in state there: 'This folly and profusion so far provoked the people that they threw dirt in the night on his escutcheon that was placed over the great gate of Somerset House.' Cromwell's body was so badly embalmed that it had to be buried quietly (the official funeral took place a fortnight later). Admiral Blake and Elizabeth Cromwell (daughter of Oliver) also lay in state. There was a small garrison based in the house, and after Richard Cromwell's abdication, Parliament unsuccessfully tried to sell the house to pay the Army. In February 1660, the garrison mutinied and surrendered to General Monck. Following his own death in 1670, Monck, now Duke of Albermarle, also lay in state in Somerset House.

Southampton House, Bloomsbury Square (TQ 3016 8178)
Built in 1637 for the 4th Earl of Southampton, Thomas Wriothesley, it was located on the north side of Bloomsbury Square. In the grounds of the house to the north were the remains of Southampton Fort, built in 1643 as part of London's Civil War defences. These remains were included in the landscaping of the gardens and remained a feature until the mid 18th century. The house was demolished in 1800. Nos. 18–27 Bloomsbury Square were built on the site of the house, whilst the site of the gardens are now covered by Bedford Place and the southern half of Russell Square.

St Andrew's Church, Holborn Circus (TQ 3135 8154)
First mentioned in 951, much of the church was rebuilt during the 15th century. During the Civil War its rector, John Hackett, continued to use the Book of Common Prayer, but was challenged by Parliamentarian soldiers

who entered the church and put a pistol to the rector's head. Hackett responded by saying 'I'm doing my duty. Now do yours'. They left without harming him. The church survived the Great Fire, but was damaged during the Second World War.

St Ann Blackfriars, **Ireland Yard (TQ 3166 8108)**
St Ann Blackfriars was established in the 16th century and destroyed in the Great Fire, although the site was retained for burials and is now occupied by Ireland Yard. In the 17th century, the church was a Puritan stronghold and for 46 years the minister was William Gouge, who died in 1653, and was buried in the church. Also buried here is Bridget, the eldest daughter of Oliver Cromwell, who died in 1681.

St Anne and St Agnes', Gresham Street (TQ 3296 8079)
The church was rebuilt in 1548 (the original 12th century church burnt down), and the tower repaired in 1629–30. In 1649, the vicar was beheaded for protesting against the execution of Charles I. Destroyed by the Great Fire, it was rebuilt by Wren and was badly damaged during the Blitz. It was rebuilt in 1963–68.

St Benet Paul's Wharf, Queen Victoria Street (TQ 3189 8096)
St Benet Paul's Wharf is the City of London's 'Welsh' church. The archaeologist and antiquarian Elias Ashmole (1617–92) was married here in 1638 (he is buried in St Mary's, Lambeth). Inigo Jones died on 21 June 1652 and was buried here alongside his parents. Destroyed in the Great Fire, it was rebuilt by Wren and the rebuilt church contains a memorial to Inigo Jones.

St Bride's, Fleet Street (TQ 3143 8118)
Thanks to the investigations of Professor Grimes in the 1940s, we know that the site occupied by the present church was originally a Roman House, and the first church was founded here in the 6th century by St Bridget. The 15th century church was closely connected with the growth of printing in Fleet Street, attracting writers and poets. Pepys was christened in St Brides and Richard Lovelace, Evelyn, Dryden, Milton and Izaak Walton were all parishioners. Lovelace was buried here in 1658 and Mary Firth, known as 'Moll Cutpurse', was buried here in 1659. Destroyed in The Great Fire, it was rebuilt by Wren in 1672.

St Clare Minoresses without Aldgate **(TQ 3354 8110)**
From the middle of the 16th century, the former Convent of the Poor Clares became a residence for the Lieutenant General of the Ordnance. From York in 1642 Charles I ordered Sir John Heydon, Lieutenant General of the Ordnance, 'to send by sea hither or to Newcastle, in as much as it will not be safe to do so by land such cannon, arms, powder, shot and munition you can get out of our stores, ships or other-wise in such secret and close manner that the same may not be interrupted by those who wish not well to our safety and person.' Heydon did so and then shortly afterwards led to join the King's army as Lieutenant General of Artillery. The armoury was

CIVIL WAR LONDON

A view of one of the remaining bastions from London's Medieval City Wall. In the background is the church of St Giles-without-Cripplegate: Oliver Cromwell was married here in 1620. (David Flintham)

closed in 1673. St Clare Street commemorates the convent.

St George the Martyr, Borough High Street (TQ 3239 7986)
Dating from the 12th century, it was rebuilt in the 14th century, and repaired in 1629. General Monk was married here in 1653, and according to Anthony à Wood, following his death in September 1658, Cromwell's body was met here by friends, clergy and gentry who accompanied it to Somerset House for its laying in state. John Rushworth, former Secretary to the Army, was buried near the pulpit of the old church in 1690. The church was rebuilt in 1734–6.

St Giles in the Fields, St Giles High Street (TQ 2984 8131)
The 12th century church was rebuilt in the 1630s, but by the end of the decade, St Giles' parishioners petitioned Parliament about what they claimed to be 'popish reliques' and as a result, the church vestry was ordered to dispose of its statues and tapestries, and remove the stained glass. Between 1640–43, two successive rectors were ejected from the parish and subsequently imprisoned on charges of ritualism. The church was rebuilt in 1733, but incorporated monuments and fittings from the earlier church. Those buried here include the diplomat Edward Herbert (d. 1648), Sir Thomas Widdrington, speaker of the 2nd Protectorate Parliament (d. 1664), Richard Penderell (who helped Charles II to escape after the Battle of Worcester, and died in 1672), and the poet, Andrew Marvell (d. 1678).

St Giles-without-Cripplegate, Fore Street (TQ 32240 81747)
Built around 1100, it was rebuilt in 1390 and in 1545. Cromwell married Elizabeth Bourchier here on 22 August 1620 and John Milton was buried here in 1674. The church contains memorials to a number of notables including Cromwell, Milton, Defoe, the mapmaker John Speed and John Bunyan.

THE GAZETTEER OF CIVIL WAR LONDON

The memorial in St Helen's Church to Martin Bond, who died in 1643. Bond's career in the London Trained Bands stretched as far back as the Armada crisis of 1588. (David Flintham)

St Gregory by Paul's, **St Paul's Churchyard (TQ 3178 8119)**
First mentioned in 1010, in 1641 enraged parishioners brought Inigo Jones before the House of Lords for partly demolishing the church to make way for the portico of St Paul's Cathedral. In 1658 the rector, Dr John Hewet, was beheaded on Tower Hill for collecting money for the exiled Charles II. The church was destroyed in the Great Fire and not rebuilt.

St Helen's, Bishopsgate (TQ 332 812)
Great St Helens dates to the 11th century (possibly 1010) and was joined in 1204 by a Benedictine nunnery built alongside. The church contains a monument to Martin Bond (d. 1643), who was with the Trained Bands at Tilbury in 1588. The memorial features soldiers in uniforms from the 1640s. The church also contains a number of defaced brasses, but these were not reckless acts of vandalism: instead, as the parish accounts identify, 'defacing the superstitious inscriptions' was a sanctioned act of iconoclasm.

St James's Palace, Cleveland Row (TQ 2910 8007)
Built by Henry VIII, The future Charles II (1630) and James II (1633) were both born and baptised at St James's, as were Mary of York (Mary II), Anne of York (Queen Anne) and James Francis Edward Stuart (the Old Pretender). The Duke of York (the future James II) was held captive between 1645 and 1648 (before escaping during a game of hide and seek in the palace gardens), whilst his father spent the night before his execution here. The palace was used as a barracks during the Commonwealth.

St James's Park (TQ 294 798)
Taking its name from the former St James's Hospital, the park was turned into formal gardens by James VI/I, who also established an aviary and a

St James's Palace: the future Kings Charles II and James II were both born here, and it was here that their father spent his last night on earth. (David Flintham)

menagerie here, as well as a physic garden. On the day of his execution Charles I was escorted across the park, his dog, Rogue, running after him. Sir Thomas Herbert recalls 'the park had several companies of foot drawn up, and a guard of halberdiers in company went, some before, and some followed; the drums beat, and the noise was so great as one could hardly hear what another spoke'. Neglected during the Commonwealth, most of the remaining trees were cut down by citizens for fuel.

St John's Churchyard, Wapping High Street (TQ 3447 8014)

Built in 1617, the church of St John the Baptist was lost to enemy bombing during the Second World War. Following his death in Doncaster on 29 October 1648 the body of the Leveller Thomas Rainsborough was brought home to Wapping, the place of his birth, for burial. His funeral on 14 November 1648 turned into a major Leveller demonstration, with thousands of mourners wearing the Levellers' ribbons of sea-green and bunches of rosemary for remembrance in their hats. Rainsborough's remains lie somewhere in St John's Churchyard and on 12 May 2013, a memorial plaque was unveiled by Tony Benn.

St Katharine Cree, Leadenhall Street (TQ 3341 8114)

Dating from 1280, the church was rebuilt in 1500–04 and again in 1628–31 (it was reconsecrated by Archbishop Laud – the 'popish' manner of this service was brought against him at his trial). The church, which survived the Great Fire, has a wooden statue of Charles I in the nave. The Laud Chapel, today furnished by the Society of King Charles the Martyr, is at the south-east corner of the church.

St Margaret's, Parliament Square (TQ 2998 7960)

Founded around the middle of the 12th century, it was rebuilt between 1486 and 1523 (and restored many times since). In 1643, it was here that MPs accepted the Solemn League and Covenant which, in return for military aid from Scotland, demanded the reform of the Church of England along Presbyterian lines. In 1647, the churchwardens were fined for observing Christmas. In 1654, 1656 and 1659, the Lord Protector and his Councillors attended services to mark the opening of three Protectorate Parliaments. Barbara Villiers, Duchess of Cleveland was christened in 1641, Pepys was married in 1655, and a year later, Milton married Katherine Wood (she was buried in the church in 1658). Also buried in the church is Wenceslaus Hollar (d. 1677). In 1661, the bodies of a number of leading Parliamentarians (including John Pym, d. 1643, John Meldrum, k. 1645, Isaac Dorislaus, k.

1649, Edward Popham, d. 1651, Richard Deane, k. 1653, Elizabeth Cromwell, d. 1654, Jane Cromwell, d. 1656, and Robert Blake, d. 1657) were exhumed and buried in a pit in the churchyard; their final resting place is now marked by a commemorative stone set in the west wall of the church, which was erected by the Cromwell Association.

St Mary Matfelon, **Whitechapel (TQ 3400 8152)**
Popularly known as St Mary's, Whitechapel, St Mary Matfelon dates from the 13th century. The third and final church was built on the site in the 19th century but was destroyed by enemy bombing on 29 December 1940 and finally demolished in 1952. Its site became St Mary's Gardens in 1966 and is now Altab Ali Park – an outline of the footprint of the church is all that remains of it. The church was the burial place of Richard Brandon, the Common Hangman of London who in 1649 beheaded the Earl of Holland and the Duke of Hamilton and was probably the person who executed King Charles I. The register of St Mary Matfelon records '1649. June 2. Richard Brandon, a man out of Rosemary Lane' (Rosemary Lane is the modern Royal Mint Street). Added to this was the following memorandum: 'This R. Brandon is supposed to have cut off the head of Charles I'. Richard Brandon was the son of Gregory Brandon, and claimed the headman's axe by inheritance – he was even known as 'Young Gregory'. The first person Young Gregory beheaded was the Earl of Strafford in 1641.

The High Anglican church of St Katherine Cree. The Laud Chapel is at the south-east corner of the church. (David Flintham)

St Nicholas Cole Abbey, Queen Victoria Street (TQ 3199 8101)
Said to be the first church to be rebuilt by Wren following the Great Fire, the pre-Fire church was a Puritan stronghold and was under the patronage of Colonel Francis Hacker, who commanded the guard at the execution of Charles I. Hacker was executed on 19 October 1660 and buried within the church.

St Paul's, Covent Garden (TQ 3017 8089)
St Paul, designed by Inigo Jones and built between 1631 and 1633, was the first new Anglican Church to be built after the Reformation. Consecrated in 1638, it was given its own parish in 1645. In 1680, both Samuel Butler (author of *Hudibras*) and the artist Peter Lely were buried here.

St Paul's Cathedral **(TQ 3200 8119)**
The fourth church on the site was built in 1087 and extended and improved during the Middle Ages before being renovated by Inigo Jones in 1633–41. Six hundred feet in length and with height of somewhere between 460 and 520 feet (its spire was destroyed by lightning in 1561), it was the scene of anti-Catholic rioting in 1549. Sir Anthony van Dyck was buried here in 1641. The Civil War interrupted the restoration work (the £17,000 remaining in the

CIVIL WAR LONDON

The memorial erected by the Cromwell Association marks the final resting place of a number of leading Parliamentarians in the churchyard of St Margaret's Church, Westminster. (David Flintham)

the nave was sold with the result that the roof fell in, and in 1647 the Bishop's Palace was demolished. In April 1649 the Leveller, Robert Lockyer was executed by firing squad outside the cathedral. By the end of the Civil Wars, the cathedral had fallen into decay. During the 1650s Sir William Dugdale detailed St Pauls, recording its monuments and epitaphs, and in 1666 the cathedral was destroyed in the Great Fire.

St Paul's Cross (TQ 3198 8124)
The cross in front of the Cathedral was demolished by order of Parliament in 1643.

St Peter Ad Vincula, The Tower of London (TQ 3345 8064)
The Chapel Royal of St Peter ad Vincula is the parish church of the Tower of London. Dating from 1520, it is situated within the Tower's Inner Ward. The remains of the regicide John Okey were interned within the church following his execution in 1662. It is recorded that as Okey had confessed his own culpability in death of King Charles I that, once executed, King Charles II had agreed to return the body to his wife for burial. But fearful that the funeral might become an anti-Restoration protest, Okey's body was instead interred within the precincts of the Tower with the minimum of burial observances.

St Saviour and St Mary Overie, Southwark (TQ 3256 8036)
Built between 1106 and 1538, it was from the tower of St Saviour's that Wenceslaus Hollar drew his *Long View of London from Bankside* in 1647. There is a memorial to Hollar in the south transept. At the Restoration the then minister, John Crodacott, opposed the reinstitution of Christmas and was finally ejected for refusing to accept the new Prayer Book. The church became Southwark Cathedral in 1905.

St Stephen Coleman, Coleman Street (TQ 3248 8134)
Dating from the 13th century, it was a Low Church stronghold during the Civil War. Communion was only allowed to those thought to be virtuous enough by a committee comprising the vicar and 13 parishioners (among them were two of the judges who condemned Charles I in 1649). It was said that it was to St Stephen's that the Five Members found refuge in January 1642. Destroyed in the Great Fire and rebuilt by Wren, it was bombed in

THE GAZETTEER OF CIVIL WAR LONDON

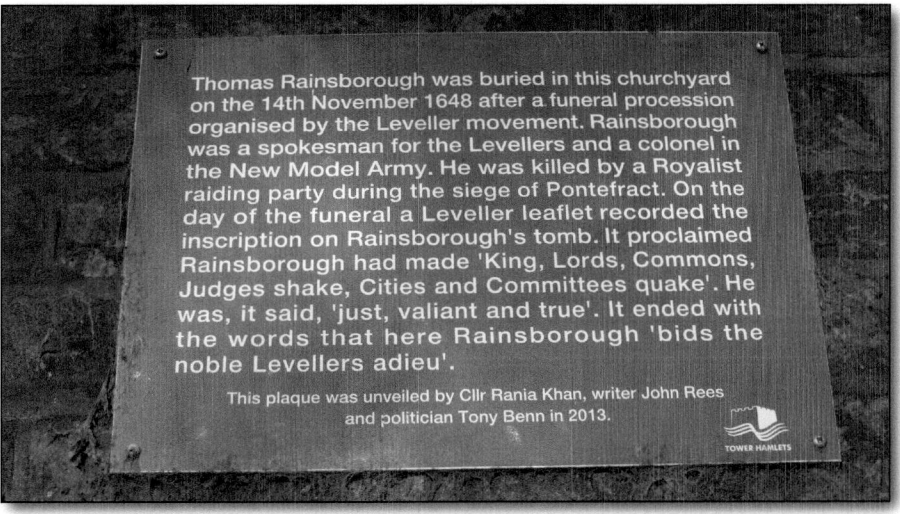

Thomas Rainsborough's remains lie somewhere in St John's Churchyard and on 12 May 2013, this memorial plaque was unveiled by Tony Benn. (David Flintham)

1940 and then demolished.

St Stephen's Chapel, **Palace of Westminster (TQ 3015 7968)**
St Stephen's Chapel was founded by Edward the Confessor, rebuilt by Edward I and finished by Edward III. During the Reformation it was secularised and by 1550 it had become the meeting place of the Commons. On Tuesday, 4 January 1642, Charles I entered St Stephen's demanding the arrest of five members of Parliament. The five members having been forewarned had fled. The King asked the speaker, William Lenthall, where the five members were. Lenthall replied 'I have neither eyes to see, nor tongue to speak in this place, but as this House is pleased to direct me'. Left with no alternative, the King withdrew. Since that day, no monarch can set foot in the Commons Chamber. The chapel was destroyed in the fire of 1834.

Statue of John Milton, City of London School (TQ 3141 8090)
Nearly opposite Blackfriars Bridge, this figure of the poet was erected in 1882 and is situated at first-floor level.

Statue of King Charles I, Banqueting House (TQ 3003 8014)
The lead bust, by an unknown sculptor, was placed over the entrance in 1950.

Statue of King Charles I, St Margaret's (TQ 3003 7960)
This lead bust by an unknown sculptor over the east door was placed here in 1949. The bust faces Thornycroft's statue of Cromwell.

Statue of King Charles I, Trafalgar Square (TQ 2992 8042)
Dating from 1633, Hubert Le Sueur's bronze equestrian statue was ordered by the then High Treasurer, Lord Weston, but not erected. Following Charles' execution in 1649, John Rivett, a brazier, was ordered to destroy it but instead buried in his garden and made a fortune by selling souvenirs allegedly made from the metal. He refused to give the statue up to Lord Weston's son in 1660, and either by gift or by purchase it came into the hands of Charles II. It was

CIVIL WAR LONDON

Hubert Le Sueur's equestrian statue of King Charles I. (David Flintham)

erected on its present site, the site of Charing Cross, in 1675, atop of a pedestal designed by Wren and carved by Grinling Gibbons. Every year on 30 January, the anniversary of the King's execution, the Royal Stuart Society lays a wreath at the statue.

Statue of Oliver Cromwell, Westminster Hall (TQ 3007 7959)
Sir Hamo Thornycroft's bronze statue dates from 1899. Cromwell carries a Bible in one hand and a sword in the other. After strong opposition by Irish MPs Parliament declined to pay for it, and so Lord Roseberry, who was the Prime Minster when the statue was first proposed, paid for it himself.

Strand (TQ 303 807)
Strand comes from the old-English for 'strand-line' or shoreline. Linking the City of London with Westminster, it became a popular location for the town houses of members of the aristocracy who needed to be close to the Court and Parliament, their names commemorated by the streets leading off the Strand: Arundel Street (Arundel House), Bedford Street (Bedford House), Buckingham Street (the owners of York House), Durham House Street (Durham Place), Exeter Street (Exeter House), and Northumberland Avenue (Northumberland House). The only houses not commemorated are Wimbledon House and Worcester House. The house next door to Northumberland House was the official residence of the Secretary of State, and during the reign of Charles I this was Sir Henry Vane. The Strand is also home to one of London's oldest pubs, the *Wig and Pen*, which dates from 1625 (alas, this is now a restaurant).

Temple Bar (TQ 3099 8115 (original site); TQ 3185 8124 (current location)
Dating from 1293, this was an outer gateway at the point where Fleet Street met the Strand. Rebuilt in 1351, during the 1630s Inigo Jones drew up plans for a new gate, but these were never carried out. Surviving the Great Fire, it was rebuilt by Wren in 1669–72 at the behest of Charles II. Taken down in 1878, the Wren gateway was rebuilt in Theobalds Park (Hertfordshire) and was then moved to Paternoster Square in 2001. It is the only surviving City gateway: Aldersgate, Aldgate, Bishopsgate, Cripplegate, Ludgate, Moorgate and Newgate had all been demolished by the end of the 18th century.

Temple Church, Temple (TQ 3114 8113)
John Selden was a jurist and a scholar of England's ancient laws and constitution. He was a member of the Long Parliament, opposing the resolution against episcopacy and later joined in the protestation of the Commons for the maintenance of the Protestant religion according to the doctrines of the Church

of England, the authority of the Crown, and the liberty of the subject. Ultimately concluding that Charles was certainly acting illegally, in the end he supported Parliament against King Charles, although Selden was not certain if Parliament was also acting illegally doing the same. He died on 30 November 1654 at Friary House in Whitefriars, and was buried in the Temple Church – his tomb is visible through glass plates in the floor.

Three Tuns, **Guildhall Yard** (TQ 3236 8137)
In February 1660, General Monck made his headquarters in this tavern upon his arrival in London.

Tothill Fields (TQ 295 789)
Tothill Fields (from where Tothill Street takes its name) was the site of the homes of aristocratic families in the 16th and early 17th centuries. In August 1643 newly raised troops of cavalry were mustered here, and according to *The London Burial Grounds* (1896), Tothill Fields served as a burial ground for over 1,000 Scottish prisoners of war and their wives captured during the Civil War (probably after the Battle of Worcester in 1651). They were interred here and in the nearby churchyard of St Margaret's. In about 1658, much of the street was rebuilt with smaller houses, some of which were used as inns.

Sir Hamo Thornycroft's bronze statue of Oliver Cromwell, dating to 1899. The statue stands outside Westminster Hall. (David Flintham)

Tower Hill, Trinity Square (TQ 3337 8076)
The site was the principle place of execution for prisoners held in the Tower of London. Some 125 people were recorded as having been executed here between 1381 and 1780 (the permanent scaffold was erected during the reign of Edward IV); most notable during the 1640s were Thomas Wentworth, Earl of Strafford (1641) and Archbishop Laud (1645). A stone set in the pavement at the west end of Trinity Square now marks the site.

Tower of London (TQ 335 806)
The Tower of London was built to command London. Yet, in 1600, more than five centuries after construction commenced, Baron Waldstein felt that the Tower intimidated Londoners as much as it did when first constructed, noting that the roof of the White Tower mounted '16 cannon which are trained upon the City'. Inigo Jones' improvements to the Tower during the 1630s included strengthening the roof of the White Tower, increasing its capacity to 21 guns, including demi-culverins and a saker. When appointed Constable of the Tower in May 1640, Lord Cottingham immediately set about strengthening its defences. He increased the size of the

CIVIL WAR LONDON

The site of Tower Hill scaffold. The Earl of Strafford and Archbishop William Laud were among those executed here. (David Flintham)

garrison to 200 men and increased the stocks of ammunition. With much of the City now within range of the Tower's guns, it was not for nothing that Edward Hyde, later Earl of Clarendon, commented that the Tower 'was looked upon as a bridle upon the city'.

Notwithstanding the Tower's dominance over London, its chief importance to both King and Parliament was as an arsenal, 'the great Magazine of the Kingdom'. In 1635, for instance, it was recorded that the Tower stored more than 2,100 barrels of gunpowder and 26,000 cannonballs. The nearby Minories, formally the convent of the Poor Clares and since converted into armories and workshops, was part of London's substantial armaments industry. In the spring of 1642, the arms and ammunition which had been stored at Berwick-upon-Tweed during the Bishops' Wars against Scotland were moved to the Tower, replenishing the stocks which had been shipped to Ireland the previous February.

In the spring of 1641 it held the first of many notable prisoners to be held there during the Civil War period, the Earl of Strafford, who was held under sentence of death following an Act of Attainder. The first of the so-called 'Army Plots' failed to free Strafford mainly thanks to the fact that the Lieutenant of the Tower, Sir William Balfour, refused to admit the plotters. However, the fact that the Tower might be seized by Royalists in a coup was not taken lightly, and the threat was made more serious in December 1641 when the King replaced Balfour with Thomas Lunsford, an appointment so unpopular that, reacting to the objections, the King gave way and four days later appointed the more acceptable Sir John Byron instead. The King knighted Lunsford, appointing him commander of an unofficial royal guard at the Palace of Whitehall, and he guarded the King during his attempt to arrest the Five Members in January 1642. Although Parliament had taken control of Westminster by the second week of January 1642, the Tower remained in Royalist (albeit moderate) hands. So Parliament decided to act. On 12 January 1642, Skippon brought a force of 500 men before the Tower in what was in effect the first 'siege' of the English Civil War. Although he

THE GAZETTEER OF CIVIL WAR LONDON

Left: The Tower of London. During the Civil Wars it was most importantly an arsenal and a prison. (David Flintham)

Below: A 19th century plan of the Tower of London, also showing the position of the scaffold at Tower Hill.

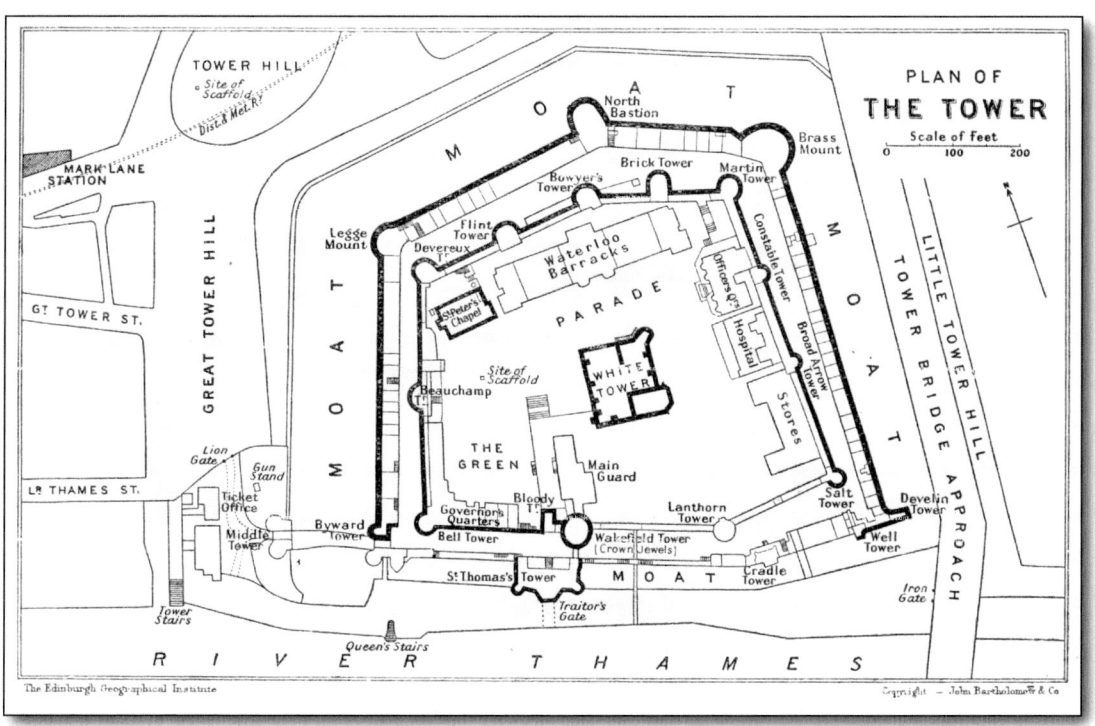

failed to get inside, the blockade made Byron's position so difficult that the King agreed to the appointment of Sir John Conyers, the preferred choice of the House of Commons, as his replacement. Thus with minimal shedding of blood did Parliament gain control of the Tower and all its military resources, and was garrisoned by the Trained Bands of the eastern suburbs.

It was from the Tower that Parliament was able to equip its artillery train with 22 pieces of ordnance in September 1642, although the Tower's remaining resources were meager as a result (even with the inflow of weapons taken from suspected Royalists). But this shortfall was addressed through imports from France and Holland, funded by City merchants. Whilst a shortage of guns could be made good, a shortage of gunners was a different matter, and with both guns in the Tower and in the new batteries being constructed to defend the main roads into London, 10 gunners were sent back to London from the Earl of Essex's artillery train. But nevertheless, during the early part of the war, London was short of trained artillerymen. The Tower remained Parliament's main arsenal, supplying its armies with powder and match, and more specialist weaponry such as petards (demolition charges). Arms, munitions, uniforms and equipment manufactured in London, and elsewhere, would be delivered to the Tower to be then shipped onto the various Parliamentarian armies.

Under Cromwell, the Crown Jewels were removed, melted down and sold, whilst both the Jewel House and the old Royal Palace were demolished. In 1651, Dutch ambassadors visited the Tower, one of them found it to be 'oddly enough not strong. Apart from the high square tower, it has no other beautiful building; for the rest is like a small town'. The Dutch artist William Schellinks visited the Tower just after the Restoration, and noted 'a lot of large and small cannons, mortars, grenades and other war materials lying around'. Thomas Venner, more famous for his failed rising in 1661, was employed as a Master Cooper in the Tower of London and in 1655 talked about blowing it up (and in April 1657 he was one of a group of about 25 Fifth Monarchists captured at Mile End Green whilst planning a rebellion).

Prisoners in the Tower

As well as being the kingdom's greatest arsenal the Tower was also a prison. From the Earl of Strafford in 1641 to General John Lambert in 1660, many of the period's leading protagonists were incarcerated in the Tower. Whilst at the outbreak of the war, the Tower held just 14 prisoners, 15 years later the Royalist writer James Howell wrote in his *Londinopolis* (1657) 'in the reign of the long Parliament, and ever since, the Tower of London hath had more number of Prisoners, than it has in the compass of a hundred years before'. It has been estimated that about one third of the entire House of Lords were imprisoned at one time or another during the 1640s and 1650s.

Imprisoned in the Tower on 25 November 1640, Thomas Wentworth, Earl of Strafford was sentenced to death by a Bill of Attainder and was executed on Tower Hill on 12th May 1641.

Sent to the Tower on 1 March 1641, Archbishop William Laud was the Tower's most distinguished prisoner during the First Civil War. He was executed following a Bill of Attainder on 10 January 1645. It is said that Strafford's ghost visited Laud on the night before his execution.

Bishop Matthew Wren, uncle of Christopher Wren and a staunch supporter of Laud, was imprisoned in the Tower between 1641 and 1659, making him the longest serving prisoner during the period. During his time in the Tower, he befriended George Monck.

Imprisoned in the Tower during the 1630s, the Parliamentarian William Prynne was vindictive in his prosecution of Archbishop Laud in 1644. At the Restoration, Prynne was appointed keeper of records at the Tower of London.

Lieutenant of the Tower for just four days in December 1641, the Royalist Sir Thomas Lunsford was captured at the siege of Hereford in December 1645. He remained a prisoner in the Tower until 1648, when he emigrated to Virginia.

The leading London Royalist Sir George Strode attempted to proclaim the commission of array (the mechanism the King used to muster armed support) in London in June 1642. Arrested, he was imprisoned in the Tower.

Sir Richard Gurney was London's leading Royalist. A former lieutenant of the Tower, he became Lord Mayor in 1641. In August 1642, he was ejected him from the mayoralty and sent to the Tower, where he lingered for seven years until he died on 6 October 1647.

Captured at the Battle of Nantwich, George Monck was confined in St Thomas's Tower for two and a half years, during which time he wrote *Observations upon Military and Political Affairs*, a military textbook stressing the importance of supply and intelligence. Released in 1646, he became a leading Commonwealth general, and masterminded the Restoration in 1660.

The Parliamentarian Sir John Hotham was imprisoned in the Tower along with his son in 1643 for attempting to betray Hull to the King. He was executed on 3 January 1645.

The Royalist poet Edmund Waller was incarcerated in the Tower in May 1643 for his part in the failed Royalist conspiracy known as 'Waller's Plot'. The fact that he was a distant cousin of Cromwell probably save his life as whilst his fellow conspirators, Richard Challoner and Nathaniel Tomkins (Waller's brother-in-law) were both executed on 5 July 1643, In November 1643 Waller was released and banished from the country.

In January 1644 Sir Basil Brooke, Master Riley and Master Violet imprisoned in the Tower after the failure of 'Brooke's Plot'.

Sir Andrew Carew was another Parliamentarian who attempted to betray a Parliamentarian stronghold to the King. Carew was sent to the Tower following his failed attempt to hand Plymouth to the King. He was subsequently executed on Tower Hill. His younger brother was executed at the Restoration as a regicide.

The Leveller John Lilburne was imprisoned in the Tower on three occasions, 1647, 1649 (on this occasion alongside William Walwyn, Richard Overton and Thomas Prince) and in 1653–54.

It is likely that Henry Rich, Earl of Holland, was held in the Tower after his capture in St Neots (Huntingdonshire) in July 1648. Despite the efforts of his brother the Earl of Warwick and Lord General Fairfax, he was sentenced to death and executed outside Westminster Hall on 9 March 1649.

John Poyer, the mayor of Pembroke, turned his back on Parliament and declared for the King in March 1648. Captured at the fall of Pembroke Castle on 11 July 1648, Poyer, Rowland Laugharne and Rice Powell, the two other Royalist commanders, were sent to the Tower. Tried for treason, their fate was decided by drawing lots – Poyer was executed by firing squad in Covent Garden and was buried in St Margaret's churchyard, Westminster.

The commander of the Scottish forces in Ireland, Robert Monro, was sent to the Tower following his capture at the fall of Carrickfergus Castle in 1648. He remained there until 1654.

The Royalist Arthur, Lord Capel was captured at Colchester in August 1648. Imprisoned in the Tower, he escaped but was betrayed and recaptured. He was executed in New Palace Yard, Westminster, on 9 March 1649.

Lord Mayor Abraham Reynardson was imprisoned in the Tower in March 1649 for refusing to make public the act proclaiming the abolition of the Monarchy.

In 1650 the Royalist poet and playwright Sir William Davenant was made lieutenant governor of Maryland, but was captured at sea, imprisoned in the Tower, and sentenced to death. Thanks to the intervention of John Milton he escaped execution but spent all of 1651 in the Tower, and was released the following year.

In August 1651 the Scottish General Alexander Leslie, Earl of Leven, was captured in Scotland, sent to London and confined to the Tower. He was later released and lived out his remaining years on his estate in Fife.

The Covenanter-turned-Royalist John Middleton commanded the Royalist horse at the Battle of Worcester (3 September 1651). Captured and sent to the Tower, he escaped and joined Charles II in exile in Paris.

Edward Massey, the former governor of Gloucester, changed his allegiance and fought for Charles II. Captured after the Battle of Worcester, he was imprisoned in the Tower of London. He escaped to Holland, but was imprisoned again when he returned to England to participate in Booth's Uprising of 1659. He escaped again and went into hiding in London, where he encouraged the soldiers' mutiny over pay on 1 February 1660.

Hugh Dubh O'Neill, who had given Cromwell a bloody nose at Clonmel in 1650, was imprisoned in the Tower following the fall of Limerick in October 1651. Because of his earlier service in the Spanish Army of Flanders, the Spanish Ambassador argued that Hugh Dubh was a Spanish subject, and so he was subsequently released into Spanish custody.

The Royalist inventor Edward Somerset, 2nd Marquis of Worcester, was imprisoned in the Tower on his return from exile in Paris in 1652. He was released in 1654.

In May 1654 Peter Vowell was imprisoned in the Tower for his part in an attempt on Cromwell's life. He was executed on 10 July.

In 1654, with Cromwell's 'Western Design' (against Spanish possessions in the Caribbean) heading for failure, the expedition's naval commander, William Penn, and its commander on land, Robert Venables, were both committed to the Tower.

In autumn 1654 Colonel Robert Overton, commander of the Commonwealth's forces in northern Scotland, was imprisoned in the Tower on Cromwell's orders, where he remained until the end of the Protectorate.

Edward Sexby and Miles Sindercombe were two former soldiers who planned to murder Cromwell in 1656 for betraying the 'good old cause' of republicanism. The plot was discovered, and Sindercombe and the hired assassin, John Cecil, were sent to the Tower. Sindercombe took poison, whilst Sexby, captured the following year, died in the Tower in 1658.

In May 1658 two Royalist conspirators, Henry Slingsby and Doctor Hewitt, were imprisoned in the Tower prior to their execution on Tower Hill.

Although a Royalist, the 2nd Duke of Buckingham was the son-in-law of Sir Thomas Fairfax. Sent to the Tower in 1658 (because, it has been said, he was Fairfax's son-in-law), he was released on Cromwell's death. He spent two further spells in the Tower during the reign of Charles II.

Failing to halt General Monck's advance from Scotland, the Republican General John Lambert was imprisoned in the Tower in January 1660 from where he escaped. Following his recapture, he lived out the rest of his days as a prisoner in Drake's Island, Plymouth Sound, where he died in 1684.

His life saved thanks to Monck's intervention, the Republican Sir Arthur Haselrige was imprisoned in the Tower where he died on 7 January 1661

Like Sir Richard Gurney before him, the Parliamentarian MP Sir Isaac Penington had also been Lieutenant of the Tower and Lord Mayor of London. He was the main intermediary between Parliament and the City during the Civil Wars. At the Restoration, he was sentenced to life imprisonment in the Tower, where he died in December 1661.

The regicides Sir John Barkstead, Colonel John Okey and Miles Corbet were captured in the Netherlands by Sir George Downing (Downing was once the chaplain in Okey's regiment). Imprisoned in the Tower (Barkstead had been a former Lieutenant of the Tower), the three were hanged, drawn and quartered, on 19 April 1662. Okey was buried within the confines of the Tower.

Tyburn, **Marble Arch (TQ 2762 8102)**
Between 1388 and 1783, it was London's principle place of public executions, although the first permanent gallows, 'made in triangular manner' erected in June 1571. It stood about 3.5 metres (11½ ft) high, and each of its three cross-beams, about 2.5 to 3 metres (8–10 ft) long, could hang up to eight people at a time. At the end of the 17th century, about 50 offences carried the death penalty, but by 1819, there were more than 200. During the Civil War period it was most notorious for the posthumous executions of John Bradshaw (died in 1659, President of the court which tried Charles I), Cromwell and Henry Ireton (d. 1651). The bodies were gibbeted from sunrise to sunset, beheaded (probably by the common hangman, Edward Dun) and the bodies buried in a pit close to the gallows (it is suggested that this might be under Connaught Place as Cromwell's ghost has been sighted here, although another legend has it that his body was spirited away by his daughter) whilst the heads were put on display at Westminster Hall. Five regicides were also executed at Tyburn: Francis Hacker and Daniel Axtell on 19 October 1660 and John Okey, John Barkstead, and Miles Corbett on 19 April 1662. The site of the gallows is

CIVIL WAR LONDON

The site of Tyburn Tree. Bradshaw, Cromwell and Ireton were posthumously executed here in 1660. (David Flintham)

marked by a stone in a traffic island at the junctions of Edgware and Bayswater Roads, although this has recently been joined by the addition of three trees.

Vere Street Theatre, **Portugal Street** (TQ 3059 8122)
Originally a real tennis court known as Gibbon's Tennis Court, it was first used as a theatre in 1653 for an underground production of Killigrew's *Claricilla*. However, the production was broken up before it debuted, reportedly betrayed to the Army by one of the actors. Licensed as a theatre at the Restoration, it was burnt down in 1809. The Peacock Theatre now occupies the site.

Wallingford House, **Whitehall** (TQ 2992 8025)
Wallingford House stood immediately north-west of Whitehall Palace and during the late 1650s it was the meeting place of the Wallingford House Party, a group of pro-Commonwealth army officers. Demolished in the 18th century, the site is now occupied by the Old Admiralty Building.

Warwick House, **Warwick Court** (TQ 3083 8173)
On the north-side of Holborn facing Chancery Lane stood Warwick House, the town house of the Earls of Warwick. Robert Rich, the 2nd Earl (1587–1658) and the Parliamentarian admiral lived here, as did his grandson following his marriage to Frances Cromwell (1638–1720) in November 1657. Three years previously both Cromwell and Charles (II) were approached about the possibility of Frances marrying Charles; apparently Cromwell laughed at the suggestion. The house was demolished towards the end of the 17th century.

Westminster Abbey (TQ 2990 7948)
Benedictine monks first came to the site in the middle of the 10th century,

whilst the Abbey itself evolved over the 13th to 16th centuries. At his coronation on 2 February 1626, Charles I wore white which many said was unlucky. During the Civil War, Parliamentarian soldiers camped in the abbey and 'broke down the rails before the Table and burnt them in the very place in the heat of July but wretchedly profaned the very Table itself by setting about it with their tobacco and all before them'. A number of prominent Parliamentarians were buried in the Abbey and were exhumed in 1661 following the Restoration and buried in a pit in the churchyard of St Margaret's. Those exhumed from St John the Baptist's Chapel were John Pym (d. 1643), William Strode (d. 1645) and Edward Popham (d. 1651). Those exhumed from Henry VII's Chapel included Elizabeth and Jane Cromwell (Oliver Cromwell's mother and sister respectively), Richard Deane (k. 1653), Humphrey Mackworth (d. 1654), Sir William Constable (d. 1655), Robert Blake (d. 1657), and Denis Bond (d. 1658). A memorial to their memory lies beneath a carpet in the RAF Chapel. The bodies of Bradshaw, Cromwell and Ireton were also disinterred, and a small slab by the entrance to the RAF Chapel marks 'The Burial Place of Oliver Cromwell, 1658–1661'. The grave, in St John the Baptist's Chapel, of the Earl of Essex, 'the late Lord General of the Forces Raised by the Parliament of England' (d. 1646) was left undisturbed at the Restoration, as were those (in Henry VII's Chapel) of Major General Charles Worsley (d. 1656) and Cromwell's favourite daughter, Elizabeth (d. 1658). Amongst the tombs and burials within the Abbey are Monck (d. 1670), Edward Montagu, 1st Earl of Sandwich (d. 1672), Edward Hyde, Duke of Clarendon (d. 1674), Prince Rupert (d. 1682), Charles II (d. 1685), James Butler, 1st Duke of Ormonde (d. 1688), and John Dryden (d. 1700).

Westminster Cathedral, Francis Street (TQ 2924 7907)
Father John Southworth was arrested a number of times for his Catholic faith and finally in 1654 he was arrested and tried under Elizabethan anti-priest legislation. He pleaded guilty to exercising the priesthood and was sentenced to death. At his execution at Tyburn on 28 June 1654 he was hanged, drawn and quartered. The Spanish ambassador returned his corpse to Douai in France for burial. His body was buried in an unmarked grave for its protection during the French Revolution, a grave which was discovered in 1927 and his remains were returned to England, where they were interred in the Chapel of St George and the English Martyrs in Westminster Cathedral. Beatified in 1929, in 1970 he was canonised by Pope Paul VI as one of the Forty Martyrs of England and Wales.

Westminster Hall, Parliament Square (TQ 3015 7959)
Built as an extension to Edward the Confessor's Palace by William Rufus in 1097, Westminster Hall is the oldest surviving building on the Parliamentary estate (the only part of Westminster Palace to survive the fire of 1834) and its hammer-beam roof, dating from 1393, is the largest medieval timber roof in Northern Europe. In January 1649, Charles I was tried and condemned to death here, and in 1653 Cromwell was installed as Lord Protector in the Hall. After their post-mortem beheadings at the Restoration, the heads of Bradshaw, Cromwell and Ireton were placed on a 20-foot spike above the

hall. In 1685 a storm broke the pole upon which Cromwell's head stood, throwing it to the ground. After this, it belonged to various private collectors and museum owners until 25 March 1960, when it was buried at Sidney Sussex College in Cambridge, Cromwell's former college.

Whitehall (TQ 300 800)

Of Tudor original, the name originally only applied to the northern part of the present thoroughfare between Charing Cross and the Holbein Gate (the site of which was roughly parallel with the Banqueting House). The central section was known simply as 'the Street', whilst the southern section, King Street. By the 16th century it was a residential street and Cromwell lived on it in 1647. In 1649, Charles I was carried along the street in a sedan chair on his way to the first and last days of his trial in Westminster Hall. The section called Whitehall was broad enough for scaffolding to be erected outside the Banqueting House for his execution and, probably on a site close to what is now Horse Guards Parade, for a gun platform to be erected towards the end of the Civil War.

Whitehall Palace, Whitehall (TQ 300 800)

Originally known as York Place, during the reign of Henry VIII it was rebuilt to replace the Palace of Westminster as his principle residence in London. Between 1530 until 1698 (when it was destroyed by fire, only the Banqueting House surviving), it grew to be the largest palace in Europe, having more than 2,000 rooms, bigger than even the Vatican and Versailles, although it was a collection of smaller buildings rather than a single large palace. Charles I built a magnificent art collection at Whitehall, its 460+ paintings including 28 Titians and 9 Raphaels, but during the Commonwealth most of these were dispersed. In February 1650 Parliament voted Cromwell the Cockpit, the former lodgings of the late Earl of Pembroke (the Cockpit was on the western ranges of the Palace, between the Holbein and King Street Gates, a site now occupied by the Treasury building). As the seat of government during the Protectorate, Cromwell lived here as Lord Protector, and died here on 3 September 1658.

Winchester Palace, Clink Street (TQ 3246 8044)

The palace of the Bishops of Winchester for over 500 years (it was built in 1109). In 1642, when the episcopacy was suppressed by order of Parliament, it was converted into a prison for Royalists. Sir Kenelm Digby was held here, during which time he wrote his *Critical Remarks* on Sir Thomas Browne's *Religio Medici*. After five years the palace was sold to Thomas Walker of Camberwell, and at the Restoration the palace, now in a bad state of repair was returned to the see of Winchester. Most of the 13th century palace was destroyed by fire in 1814.

Wood Street (TQ 3224 8159)

On 31 July 1643 Lieutenant Colonel William Barriffe, the military theorist and author of the influential *Military Discipline*, was buried at an unknown location in Wood Street. Barriffe was a member of the Society of the Artillery

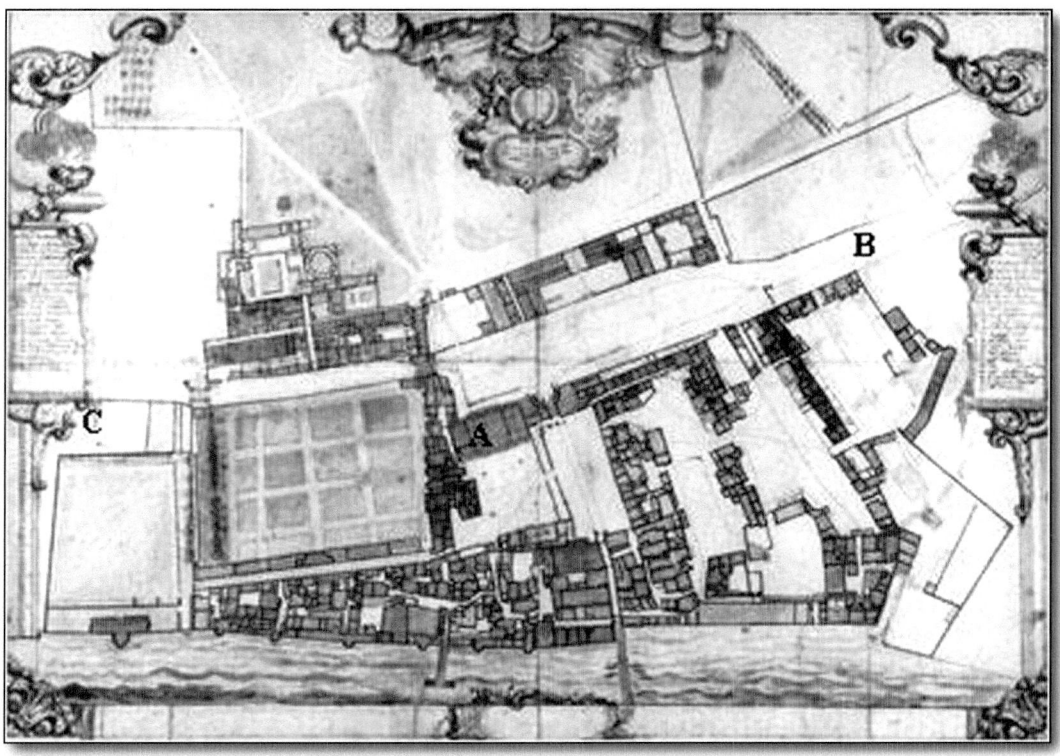

George Vertue's retrospective plan of Whitehall Palace as it had been in 1680. The Banqueting House is marked 'A' whilst the modern Whitehall cuts clean through the site of the Palace from 'B' to 'C'.

Garden and at the outbreak of the war, an officer in the Trained Bands. He served in John Hampden's regiment, and died of sickness in July 1643.

Worcester House, **Strand** (TQ 3037 8079)
In 1532, the 1st Earl of Bedford sold the former town house of the Bishop of Carlisle to the 3rd Earl of Worcester. Seized by Parliament during the Civil War, after the King's execution in 1649, it was used to store valuables. At the Restoration Lord Clarendon rented it for six years whilst his own Clarendon House was being built, and in 1660 James, Duke of York (later James VII/II) secretly married Anne Hyde, Clarendon's daughter. The house was demolished soon after 1674.

Worship Street (TQ 329 821)
A foundry, used for the casting of cannon during the Civil Wars, was leased by John Wesley the following century as a place of worship.

York House, **Strand** (TQ 3025 8052)
Built sometime before 1237, Mary I gave the house to Nicholas Heath, Archbishop of York in 1556. During the reign of James VI/I it became the residence of his favourite, George Villiers, 1st Duke of Buckingham who apparently repaired the house and built the York Watergate (this gate, leading from the house to the river steps, is all that remains of York House, and can be found on Watergate Walk, WC2). Following the Duke's murder in 1628, in 1635 his widow married Randal MacDonnell, 2nd Earl and 1st Marquis of Antrim. Confiscated during the Civil War, it became a London residence of Sir Thomas

Fairfax. In 1657 the 2nd Duke of Buckingham married Fairfax's daughter Mary, and at the Restoration the house was returned to the Buckinghams who used it for ceremonial occasions, the rest of the time leasing it to foreign ambassadors. The house was demolished in 1670, leaving only the Watergate. Villiers Street, built during the 1670s, now occupies the site.

Outside the Lines of Communication

Acton

Acton (TQ 199 802)

The town earned more than just local fame during the opening months of the English Civil War when, in November 1642, the Royalist advance on London was opposed by local Parliamentarians at Brentford. According to Daniel Lysons in *The Environs of London* (1795) 'In November 1642, a few days before the battle of Brentford, the Lord General (the Earl of Essex) and the Earl of Warwick, marching with their forces out of London, made Acton the place of their rendezvous'. The fighting at Brentford spread into Acton. Later, this was one of a number of places around London where Parliamentarian cavalry would graze their horses. Acton House, long since demolished, was home to Phillip Skippon. Maria Comes, his first wife, was buried in St Mary's Church (rebuilt in the mid 19th century). In 1651, according to Lysons, 'When Cromwell returned to London after the battle of Worcester, he was met at this place by the Lord President, the Council of State, many of the Nobility, the House of Commons, the Lord Mayor, Aldermen, and Common Council of the city of London, &c. &c. forming in the whole a train of more than 300 coaches'. Richard Baxter, the Puritan church leader, was also an Acton resident.

Blackheath

Blackheath (TQ 392 767)

On 29 May 1648, Fairfax arrived in Blackheath at the head of his army on the trail of Royalist insurgents who had recently fled Deptford and had moved on to Dartford. On 30 May there was some skirmishing between the Kentish Royalists and Colonel Rich's Horse and Colonel Barkstead's foot. Three days later Blackheath was occupied by a force of Royalists under the command of George Goring, Earl of Norwich, but with London secure against him, most of the force dispersed leaving Goring and his remaining followers to cross the Thames at Greenwich the next day.

On 1 May 1657, the troops raised for service in Flanders (following the Treaty of Alliance between England and France) were mustered on Blackheath before departing for France. Three years later, Charles II was welcomed at Blackheath on his return to London at his Restoration.

Brentford (Battle of) (TQ 1786 7750)

The Battle of Edgehill was inconclusive. The Parliamentary army under Essex retreated to London via Northampton, arriving in the capital on 7 November, whilst the King slowly advanced on London via Banbury, Oxford and Reading.

THE GAZETTEER OF CIVIL WAR LONDON

A map of modern-day Greater London identifying a number of key locations:

A: The City of London
B: The Battle of Bow Bridge (1648)
C: Blackheath / Greenwich
D: Putney
E: The Battle of Brentford (1642)
F: The Battle of Turnham Green (1642)
G: The Battle of Surbiton (1648)
H: Westminster / Whitehall
I: Hounslow Heath
J: Southwark
K: Vauxhall
L: Uxbridge
M: Hammersmith
N: Kingston-upon-Thames

On 10 November, with the Royalists deployed in a wide area to the west of London, Parliament voted to open peace negotiations with the King, and sent representatives to meet with him at Colnbrook (8 km (5 miles) east of Windsor) on 11 November. Whilst the King agreed to talks at Windsor, the Royalists had already decided to march on the capital and during the foggy morning of 12 November the Royal army assembled on Hounslow Heath. It was decided to advance along the Great West Road into London, but first the Parliamentary garrison at Brentford would have to be cleared.

Initially Prince Rupert intended to lead the assault, but General Patrick Ruthven, the Earl of Forth (who would be made Earl of Brentford in 1644), came up and took overall control of the Royalist forces, which probably totalled around 13,000. The bulk of the army advanced to Hounslow, whilst about 4,000 foot and 800 cavalry, supported by four cannons, approached Brentford. Denzil Holles's red-coated regiment (700–800 men) and Lord Brooke's purple-coated regiment (480 men) held Brentford for Parliament. They were supported by 10–12 troops of cavalry, but most of these fled at the first sight of the Royalists.

Around noon on 12 November 1642 the Royalists advanced through the heavy mist along the London Road. The Royalist vanguard, the Prince of Wales's regiment of horse, reached Sir Richard Wynn's house (TQ 1692 7700) where it was surprised by parliamentary artillery positioned behind a great hedge, and Holles's regiment which had garrisoned the house itself. The Royalists were forced to retreat until Sir Thomas Salusbury's Royalist foot regiment arrived to clear the Parliamentary pickets from the house. The Royalist advance recommenced only to find the bridge across the River Brent (TQ 1729 7729) barricaded.

One thousand Royalist musketeers attacked, and within an hour had forced the Parliamentarians at this barricade to retreat to yet another barricade (probably located on the crest of the rising ground by modern Ferry Lane – TQ 1785 7755). This barricade was defended by Brooke's regiment, plus two small cannon. Despite being faced by as many as six regiments, the defenders held on, and it was only after two to three hours of fighting, with the Royalists outflanking the position, that the Parliamentarians were finally driven from it.

The Parliamentarians were routed. Some fled through Brentford towards London, whilst others headed south and attempted to escape by swimming the Thames where many were drowned. The Royalists advanced through Brentford, but were halted when they encountered fresh parliamentary troops in an open field outside to the east of the town, probably Turnham Green or Chiswick common. These reinforcements were John Hampden's green-coated regiment of foot, and to cover the retreat of Holles's and Brooke's regiments they charged the Royalists no less than five times.

Light was now fading, and with the Royalists exhausted after more than four hours of fighting, the opposing forces disengaged, the victorious Royalists falling back on Brentford which they subsequently looted. Royalist losses were few, probably only around 20, but the Parliamentarians lost about 50 killed in the fighting and at least as many again drowned in the rout. Added to this, 21 Parliamentarian officers were captured along with 57 soldiers from Brooke's and 249 from Holles's regiments. Amongst the captives was

John Lilburne, the future Leveller leader, who fought with distinction at Brentford and his actions here may have saved the Parliamentarian artillery train, guarded by less than 100 soldiers at Hammersmith. He was sent as a prisoner to Oxford, but was later exchanged.

The final act of the battle occurred overnight, when the Parliamentarians attempted to bring arms and ammunition by barge down the Thames from Kingston to London. The barges came under musket fire from the Royalists at Syon House (TQ 1728 7666), and from artillery fire from the cannon deployed between Brentford and modern-day Kew Bridge. With little hope of escape, the crews scuttled their vessels (these were recovered once the Royalists had withdrawn). The next day two Parliamentarian vessels attacked Syon House from the Thames, causing some damage, although one boat was sunk by Royalist counterfire.

Whilst the Battle of Brentford had been a Royalist victory, the Parliamentarians had checked the King's advance and had earned them precious time to bring together forces capable of halting the King outside London. The next few days would be vital for both sides.

Bow Bridge (Battle of) (TQ 37796 83126)

Royalist activity in south-east England did not end with the defeat of Royalist forces under the Earl of Norwich at Maidstone on 1 June 1648: three days later an uprising occurred at Chelmsford and Norwich, and still hoping for Royalist support from London, they crossed the Thames at Greenwich. But finding no support close to London, they crossed Bow Bridge and headed for Chelmsford.

St Lawrence's Church, Brentford. The tower was probably used as an observation post by Holles' regiment during their defence of Brentford bridge. (David Flintham)

Although most of Norwich's army had already dispersed, on Sunday 4 June some 500 cavalry under the command of Sir William Compton remained, and these then followed across the Thames, the troopers in boats, the horses swimming alongside, intending for the Essex side of the River Lea. But whether due to poor navigation or strong tides, the Royalists were scattered, finding landfall around Stepney. Once reformed, they almost immediately came into contact with a body of foot from the Tower Hamlets Trained Bands. But after extracting a promise that the Trained Bands would disband, Compton took his Royalists to Bow Bridge (TQ 379 830) where, forcing the turnpike, they crossed the river into Essex. At Stratford the Royalists met Norwich, who had returned from Chelmsford. To counter this threat, the Parliamentarians moved two three-pounder cannon (known as 'drakes') to Aldgate, 4.5 km (2.8 miles) from Bow Bridge.

Mile End Green was an area of common ground through which ran the road to Colchester (this road crossed the Lea at Bow Bridge). In 1578 the chronicler Holinshed wrote: 'This common land was sometimes, yea, in the memorie of men yet living, a large mile long (from Whitechappell to

CIVIL WAR LONDON

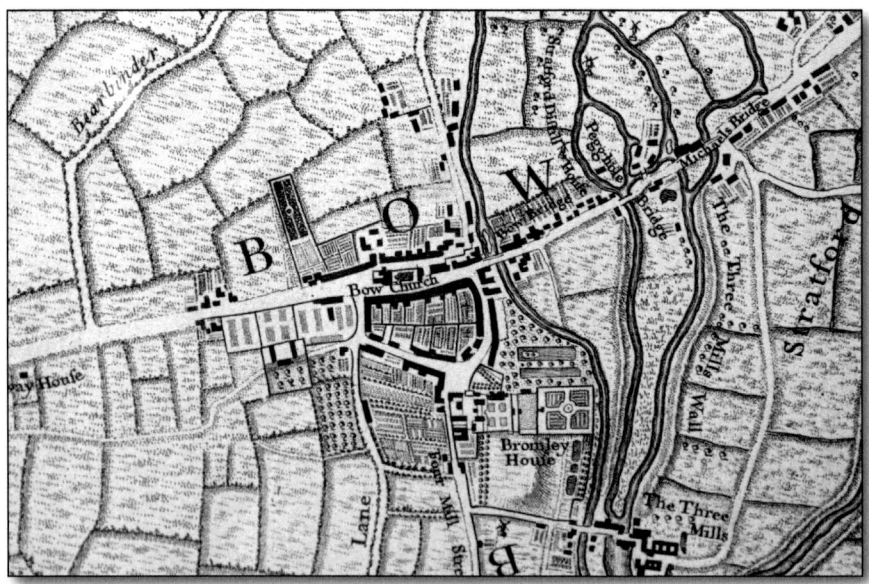

John Rocque's 1747 map of Bow – Bow Bridge and Bow Church can be clearly seen. Mile End, where the Parliamentarians advanced from is the west (left of map), whilst Stratford is to the east. (David Flintham)

Stepenheth church) and therefore called Mile-end green'. It was a place of assembly, including during the Armada crisis of 1588 when the local militia assembled on the green. All that remains today of the old common is the small remnant that survives as Stepney Green. It was on the green that Colonel Whalley assembled a force of Parliamentarian cavalry and dragoons.

The Royalists returned to Bow Bridge, encountering two companies of the Tower Hamlets Trained Bands, who immediately fled. The Royalists then barricaded Bow Bridge and installed two light cannon (also drakes), and lined nearby hedges with muskets, apparently just in time, as advancing from Mile End was Whalley and his cavalry and dragoons. According to a Parliamentarian account, at one o'clock in the afternoon Whalley advanced on Bow, but finding the Royalists in a strong position, was content to withdraw 'with two or three prisoners taken, and as many slain'. Skirmishing took place along the road between Bow and as far east as Mile End itself where, according to a Royalist account, four troops of Parliamentarian horse encountered a Royalist scouting party, who, despite being outnumbered, charged the Parliamentarians who 'began to run for it, and bid the devil take the hindmost'. According to another Royalist account, some of the Parliamentarians fled to Whitechapel, and some even as far as Temple Bar. The Parliamentarians counterattacked, and, joined by the Tower Hamlets Trained Bands, pushed the Royalists back. But at Bow Bridge, the Royalists' were reinforced and forced the trained bandsmen back on Bow Church (St Mary and Holy Trinity, TQ 3765 8297), where they took refuge and were forced to surrender on the promise that they would disband.

Casualties were light on both sides. Whilst the Royalists enjoyed the better of the fighting, and even though they had come within an hour's march of the City of London itself, Londoners again refused to rise for the King. Barricading Bow Bridge, the Royalists withdrew first to Stratford where they remained until 9 June. Here, a lack of supplies forced then to head first to

THE GAZETTEER OF CIVIL WAR LONDON

Chelmsford, and then ultimately to Colchester where they would be finally defeated following an 11 week siege.

Chelsea

Chelsea Manor House *(TQ 2729 7772)*
Built around 1536 by Henry VIII, between 1639 and 1649, the house belonged to James, Duke of Hamilton, who built a large extension to the west. The entire house was seized by Parliament in 1653.

Chiswick

Chiswick, St Nicholas' *(TQ 2155 7791)*
Only the ragstone tower remains from the medieval church, the rest was completely rebuilt in 1883, funded by Henry Smith of the local brewers Fuller, Smith and Turner. Buried in the church without memorials are two of Cromwell's daughters, Mary (d. 1713) and Frances (d. 1721). Legend has it that following his posthumous execution at Tyburn, Cromwell's headless torso was spirited away and buried in the crypt of St Nicholas.

Statue of Inigo Jones, Chiswick House *(TQ 2091 7757)*
Dating from 1729, this stone statue is by were sculpted by one of the most famous and sought after talents of the day, the Flemish sculptor Michael Rysbrack.

Croydon

Croydon Archbishop's Palace, Old Palace Road *(TQ 3186 6544)*
Built during the 14th and 15th centuries, the Archbishop's Palace was once the summer residence of the Archbishops of Canterbury. Seized by Parliament during the First Civil War, it was then acquired by Sir William Brereton, the Parliamentarian commander in Cheshire, who spent most of the 1650s there, and died there in April 1661. The palace was then returned to the church. Croydon itself was garrisoned by Parliamentarian troops after the Battle of Surbiton in July 1648.

Deptford

Deptford Dockyard *(TQ 369 782)*
Founded in 1513 by Henry VIII, Deptford Dockyard was the most significant royal dockyard in Tudor England. Seventeenth century expansion included the lengthening and enlarging of the Great Dock in 1610, whilst in 1620 a second dry dock was built, with a third being authorised in 1623. There was further investment in the Commonwealth period, with money spent on providing a mast dock and three new wharves. It remained a principal naval yard until the 1830s, by which time the new larger warships were hampered by the shallow narrow river. The yard was closed in 1869, although the victualling yard remained in use until the 1960s, while the land used by the dockyard was sold. The area is currently known as Convoys Wharf.

The memorial to the Battle of Brentford. It is located close to where Brooke's regiment were positioned during the battle on 12 November 1642. (David Flintham)

Sayes Court (TQ 3670 7808)

The manor of Sayes Court was seized by the Parliament on the execution of Charles I, who assigned it to the Browne family, who had occupied it for several generations. In 1647 Mary Browne, daughter and heir of Sir Richard Browne, married John Evelyn (whose family wealth was largely founded on gunpowder production) and he took up residence in his wife's family home in 1651. At the Restoration Evelyn managed obtained a 99 year lease of the property. Today the site and its once famous gardens are completely buried beneath Convoys Wharf, with only the run down and vandalised Sayes Court Park giving any indication of former glories.

Deptford was temporarily occupied by Royalist sympathisers on 26 May 1648, but withdraw at the news that Fairfax was mustering his army.

Dulwich

Dulwich College, College Road (TQ 3311 7285)

The fellows supported the King during the Civil War and pawned the college silver for the Royalist cause. Parliamentarian troops were quartered here and melted organ pipes and coffins for lead bullets. By the Restoration, the college was in a dilapidated state.

Eltham

Eltham Palace (TQ 4240 7418)

Following the King's execution, Parliament took possession of the palace, noting it was 'much out of repair'. Parliament sold it to Colonel Nathaniel Rich who began to demolish it. John Evelyn visited the site in 1656, noting 'Both the palace and chapel in miserable ruins, the noble wood and park destroyed by Rich the Rebel'.

Enfield

Enfield Chase (TQ 3091 9766)

There were agrarian riots in 1659 over property rights to Enfield Chase, culminating in a skirmish between local commoners and troops. During the 1650s gunpowder mills were established at *Enfield Lock* (TQ 374 991) and *Enfield Mill* (TQ 362 955)

Greenwich

Greenwich Palace (TQ 3856 7780)

A favourite residence of the Tudors, Greenwich Palace and Park was also favoured by the Queen of James VI/I, Anne of Denmark. It was under Anne that a number of improvements were made, most notably the building of the Queens House, designed by Inigo Jones. In 1652, Parliament attempted to sell the palace but could not find a buyer. It was stripped of its paintings and furniture and turned into a biscuit factory. During 1653–54, Dutch prisoners of war were kept there.

Queen's House, Greenwich (TQ 3859 7775)

In 1616 Inigo Jones was commissioned by Anne of Denmark to design

The Queen's House, Greenwich. Designed by Inigo Jones, it was a residence of Henrietta Maria until 1642. It was later used for the lying-in-state of Commonwealth generals, including Admiral Blake in 1657. (David Flintham)

a house for her, but by the time of her death three years later it had not progressed very far. Passed to Prince Charles, it was Charles's Queen, Henrietta Maria, who asked Inigo Jones to complete the house and his Palladian-style building was built 1629–40. Henrietta Maria was pleased with the building and called it her 'House of Delights'. She left London in 1642 to raise funds for arms in Holland (using the pretext of taking her 10-year-old daughter Mary to meet her betrothed, Prince William). Parliamentarian troops searched the house for arms on 3 November 1642 but found nothing, and the house itself was taken from Royal ownership. Unlike most Crown lands, Greenwich was not sold after the Civil War and was retained as a residence for the Protector, although much of the artwork was sold. Bulstrode Whitelock lived there and the house was used for the lying-in-state of Commonwealth generals, including Admiral Blake in 1657. At the Restoration, Henrietta Maria returned.

Statue of Robert Blake, Discover Greenwich Visitor Centre (TQ 3825 7793)
A bust of Robert Blake overlooks the entrance to the Old Royal Naval College.

Hammersmith
The Parliamentarian artillery was assembled in Hammersmith prior to the Battle of Turnham Green.

Brandenburgh House, **Fulham Palace Road (TQ 234 780)**
Also known as 'The Great House' it was built for Sir Nicholas Crisp during the reign of Charles I and is generally felt to have been the location of the Parsons Green hospital, established in March 1645, and was the last of

three military hospitals which was established by Parliament. Catering for both Parliamentarian and Royalist soldiers, it closed as a hospital at the end of the First Civil War. In August 1647 when the New Model Army was stationed in Hammersmith, Fairfax used it as his headquarters. In 1660, it was returned to Sir Nicholas who assisted General Monck plan the Restoration. The house was demolished in 1821.

St Paul's, Hammersmith (TQ 2318 7850)

The church dates back to the 1630s, the chapel of ease being consecrated by Archbishop Laud on 7 June 1631. The present church dates from the 1880s. Sir Samuel Morland (or Moreland) was buried here in 1695. Whilst known as an inventor, Morland was also involved in espionage. He was secretary to John Thurloe (Cromwell's 'spymaster') but became disillusioned with the Commonwealth, allegedly after learning of a plot by Sir Richard Willis, Thurloe and Richard Cromwell to assassinate the future King Charles II. He became a double agent, working towards the Restoration, engaging in espionage and cryptography. During the 1660s Morland built a fine house and gardens on the site of the old Vauxhall Manor. Another memorial is that to the London Royalist Sir Nicholas Crispe (*c.*1599–1666): with experience of trade with Africa before the war (particularly building trading forts on the Gold Coast of Komenda and Kormantin), in 1644 he was commissioned to equip 15 warships at his own expense to operate from West Country ports to Ireland and the Continent.

Hampton

Hampton Court Palace (TQ 1561 6856)

Charles I used Hampton Court Palace as a refuge from the troubles of London in the years leading up to the outbreak of the Civil War, and it was to here that Charles fled with his family in January 1642. Five years later he was held as a prisoner here, but during his absence the Puritans had desecrated the chapel, destroying 'popish and superstitious pictures and images'. A few months after Charles's execution Parliament put Hampton Court Palace up for sale, the proceeds to be sued to settle royal debts and 'for the benefit of the Commonwealth'. In 1651, however, Cromwell put a stop to the sale and in December 1653 it was given over to the new Protector and Cromwell used it has his weekend residence with his family, Cromwell himself using Charles I's former Day Rooms on the ground floor as his bedroom. At the Restoration, Charles II had the palace repaired and redecorated, and bought back many of the tapestries, pictures and items of furniture which had been sold during the Commonwealth.

Harrow-on-the-Hill

Harrow-on-the-Hill (TQ 1529 8750)

This was one of a number of places were Parliamentarian cavalry would graze their horses. On the hill there is a spot called 'King Charles's Well' and it was here, so legend has it, that the King stopped to water his horses whilst en route to surrender to the Scots Army in 1646.

Flambards, Harrow-on-the-Hill (TQ 1531 8692)
The old mansion of Flambards (or Flamberts), probably dated back to the 14th century and stood at the south end of the village of Harrow-on-the-Hill. It was home to Sir Gilbert Gerard, 1st Baronet of Harrow on the Hill (1587–1670), who sat in the House of Commons at various times between 1614 and 1660. An opponent of the Earl of Strafford, during the Civil War he raised 4,000 troops for Parliament. He was appointed to the Committee of Both Kingdoms and was made paymaster of the Parliamentarian army. As such, he had three pence in the pound allowance, which was ultimately worth in the region of £50,000. He was appointed Chancellor of the Duchy of Lancaster and was made a lord of his upper house by Cromwell. After Richard Cromwell resigned as Protector Gerard was refused admission to the House of Commons, but was later nominated as a member of the new Council of State. Surviving the Restoration, he died on 6 January 1670, and was buried in Harrow.

High Barnet
Ye Old Mitre Inne, 58 High Street, High Barnet (TQ 2453 9651)
Charles I is reputed to have stopped here en route to Oxford, and in 1660 General Monck was supposed to have stopped in the *Mitre Inn*. Off the High Street lies the site of the 17th century militia headquarters.

Highgate
Lauderdale House, Waterlow Park (TQ 2866 8728)
This house, south of Highgate Hill, on an area of 29 acres, was built in 1582. In 1641 the house was purchased by the Countess of Home, and on her death it passed to her daughter, Anne, who married John Maitland, the 2nd Earl of Lauderdale, who reconstructed the house in around 1645. Henry Ireton's brother John, lived here during the Commonwealth, and at the Restoration it was returned to Lauderdale. Lauderdale himself had intrigued against Charles I, but was a supporter of Charles II, organising his coronation at Scone on 1 January 1651 and fighting with him at Worcester on 3 September in the same year. At the Restoration he was made Duke of Lauderdale. Lauderdale House, as the house became known, was borrowed by Charles II for Nell Gwynne. The house is now and arts and education centre.

Hillingdon
Red Lion Inn, Royal Lane, Hillingdon (TQ 0671 8290)
Now called the Red Lion Hotel, Charles I halted here briefly in 1646.

Hornchurch
St Andrew's Church, Hornchurch (TQ 5405 87101)
Dating from 1222, the church contains the tomb of Thomas Witherings, Postmaster General to Charles I. Witherings was both an MP and an Alderman. It was claimed that he had assisted the Earl of Norwich in the Royalist insurrection in Essex during 1648, but the charges were dismissed. He died in August 1651.

Hounslow

Baber Bridge (TQ 1105 7460)

A water-powered sword mill was established here in 1630 by Benjamin Stone, who later became 'His Majesty's Blademaker for the office of the Ordnance'. At the outbreak of the Civil War, the mill was confiscated and turned into a gunpowder mill.

Hounslow Heath (TQ 122 743)

It was from Hounslow Heath that the Royalist army advanced to Turnham Green on 13 November 1642, and it was to Turnham Green that it retreated. Fairfax met representatives from the City of London on the Heath on 4 August 1647, whilst in May the following year Fairfax reviewed his army there before advancing into Kent. On 1 June 1650 Cromwell was officially welcomed following his return from Ireland.

Isleworth

Syon House, Isleworth (TQ 1709 7688)

Built during the reign of Edward VI on the site of a former Bridgettine monastery, since 1594 Syon House was the home of the Percys, the Earls of Northumberland. The 10th Earl employed Inigo Jones to make improvements to the house. It was garrisoned by Royalist troops during the Battle of Brentford in November 1642, and attacked by cannon-armed Parliamentarian boats, causing some damage to the house itself. In 1646 three of Charles I's children were placed under the care of the 10th Earl at Syon to escape an outbreak of plague in London. Charles I visited them here and it was during one of these visits that it is likely that Lely painted a portrait of Charles and the Duke of York. In 1647, a council was held at Syon, attended by Cromwell.

Islington

Rectory of St Mary, Upper Street, Islington (TQ 3163 8392)

Sir Arthur Haselrige lived in Islington, at the former rectory of St Mary, Islington (formerly, the convent of St Leonard). Born in 1601, Haselrige was an MP between 1640 and 1659 and famously was one of the Five Members. Upon the outbreak of war, he raised a troop of armoured cavalry or cuirassiers, later nicknamed 'Haselrige's Lobsters', for Parliament. Later, Haselrige declined to act as a judge at the trial of Kings Charles I, but approved of his execution. During the Commonwealth, he tried to uphold the republic against Cromwell's autocracy and following Cromwell's death, he opposed both John Lambert's attempted military coup and the Restoration. At the Restoration Hesilrige's life was saved by Monck's intervention, but he was imprisoned in the Tower of London where he died on 7 January 1661. Another Islington resident was Colonel John Okey, commander of the New Model Army's dragoons at the Battle of Naseby, one of the judges at the trial of Charles I in January 1649 and a signatory to the King's death warrant. Before the war he was a drayman and then a stoker at an unnamed Islington brewery. As a regicide, he fled to Holland on the Restoration but was captured and returned to London where he stood trial and was executed on 19 April 1662.

Kensington
Fox and Bull, Albert Gate, Knightsbridge (TQ 2778 7983)
A tavern dating from at least Elizabethan times. When it was demolished in 1835–36, the bodies of several Civil War soldiers were discovered.

Holland House and Park (TQ 2469 7973)
Built around 1606, this Jacobean mansion became the home of Sir Henry Rich, following his marriage to the daughter of Sir Walter Cope. Rich, later Earl of Holland, commanded a Royalist army during the 2nd Civil War, but was defeated first at Kingston-upon-Thames, and again St Neots (9 July 1648) where he was captured. He was tried, condemned to death, and executed on 9 March 1649, before Westminster Hall. Holland House was then confiscated by Parliament. It was said that Cromwell used the surrounding fields for discussions with his deaf son-in-law, Henry Ireton, so they would not be overheard by eavesdroppers. During the 1650s, the house was restored to Lady Holland who had plays privately performed here in defiance of the laws during the Commonwealth.

Kingston upon Thames
Kingston upon Thames (TQ 1778 6936)
During the 17th century Kingston-upon-Thames was the lowest crossing point of the Thames before London Bridge, and thus was strategically important to both sides. The town was garrisoned by Parliament at the outbreak of the war but was evacuated on 12–13 November 1642 before the approach of the Royalist army. It was held for the King for the next five days before the Royalists evacuated it. After the first Civil War, the Parliamentary army was frequently based in and around the town, and in 1647 Fairfax briefly used the 14th century Crane Inn (now demolished) as his headquarters. On 7 July 1648, a battle between the Earl of Holland's Royalists and a Parliamentarian force took place on nearby Surbiton Common (see the Battle of Surbiton), the defeated Royalists being pursued to Kingston where they escaped across the Thames.

River Lea
By the middle of the 17th century, the River Lea was the centre of London's gunpowder production. The river was important as it would power the watermills crucial to mill the gunpowder, and also to transport the raw materials and finished powder. From its beginnings at *St Thomas' Mills*, Stratford (TQ 379 835), by the end of the 1640s production was also underway at *Temple Mills* in Leyton (TQ 376 854). During the 1650s, mills were also set up at *Enfield Lock* (TQ 374 991), *Enfield Mill* (TQ 362 955), *Tottenham* (TQ 348 896), and *Walthamstow* (TQ 3507 8829).

Putney
Putney in 1642 was a small Thames-side town of about 900 people. A week after the Battle of Turnham Green, Parliament constructed a bridge of

boats across the Thames. When the army established its headquarters in the town in August 1647, the officers were billeted in a number of houses including Sir Thomas Fairfax in a house close to the modern railway station (TQ 23861 75153), Henry Ireton in a house on modern Putney Bridge Road (TQ 2400 7553), and Thomas Rainsborough and John Okey in two houses on Fulham Palace Road (TQ 2423 7631), north of the river.

St Mary the Virgin, Putney (TQ 2407 7565)
Although most of today's church (apart from the 15th century tower) dates from the 19th century, the church is famous for being the location of the Putney debates, the Council of War headed by Fairfax, Cromwell and Ireton in November 1647. It is said that the Cromwellian generals sat around the Communion table defiantly wearing their hats. A Cromwell Association plaque within the church commemorates the event. In November 1642, following the Battle of Turnham Green, the Parliamentarians constructed a bridge of boats across the Thames at Putney.

Ravenscourt Park
Ravenscourt Park (TQ 2232 7926)
Ravenscourt Park is the remnant of the park which was attached to the 14th century Manor House of Paddenswick. In 1631 it was purchased by Sir Richard Gurney, the Royalist Lord Mayor of London who died in the Tower in 1647. In 1650 it was purchased by Maximillian Bard, who pulled the old manor house down and replaced it with a house to the west of it.

Richmond
Ham House, Richmond (TQ 1698 7303)
Built in 1610 and relatively unaltered from the 17th century, in 1637 the house was acquired by William Murray, former whipping boy to the future Charles I (Murray would be punished for Charles's misdemeanours), but the relationship was beneficial and as a result of his subsequent friendship with the King, Murray was given a peerage (as the 1st Earl of Dysart) and the lease of the manors of Ham and Petersham. His only daughter, Elizabeth, acquired the title of Countess of Dysart, and during the Commonwealth she exercised considerable political power, influencing Cromwell and furthering the Royalist cause. She later married John Maitland, Earl of Lauderdale.

Richmond Park (TQ 1899 7337)
Enclosed by Charles I in 1637 to provide a hunting ground close to Hampton Court and Richmond Palace, in 1649 the park was given to the City of London by the Commonwealth Government in return for its support during the Civil Wars. It was returned to Charles II in 1660.

Peter Pett's *Sovereign of the Seas* was constructed in 1637 in Woolwich Dockyard.

part of what is now Home Park Road, in 1638, the manor and manor house was acquired by Queen Henrietta Maria. Modified by Inigo Jones 1640–41, it was bought by John Lambert in 1652. Cromwell visited Lambert in Wimbledon several times, and after his fall from power it is where Lambert retired: 'after he had been discarded by Cromwell, betook himself to Wimbledon-house, where he turned florist, and had the finest tulips and gilliflowers that could be got for love or money; yet in these outward pleasures he nourished the ambition which he entertained before he was cashiered by Cromwell.' In 1660 the manor returned to the Crown. The house was demolished in 1717. Wimbledon itself is home to the Rose and Crown pub (TQ 23724 71197) which dates from 1659.

Woolwich

Woolwich Dockyard (TQ 4271 7924)

The Royal Dockyard was created by Henry VIII in 1512–13, and closed in 1869. Peter Pett's *Sovereign of the Seas* was constructed here in 1637. Ordered as 90 gun first-rate ship of the line, she was launched on 13 October 1637 with 102 bronze guns. She was renamed *Sovereign* in 1651 and then *Royal Sovereign* in 1685. During her service, she participated in three major sea battles in 1651 against the Dutch at the Battle of the Kentish Knock (during this battle she ran aground), against the French at Battle of Beachy Head (1690) and the Battle of La Hougue (1692). She was destroyed by fire at Chatham in 1697.

Bibliography

Primary Sources
Official Records
Calender of State Papers, Domestic, Charles I (reprinted as Hamilton, W. D. (ed.), *Calender of State Papers, Domestic Series* (London, HMSO, 1887)
Calender of State Papers, Venetian, 1642–43 (reprinted as T*he English Civil War – A Contemporary Account* (London: Caliban Books, 1996)
Corporation of London Record Office, Journals of the Court of Common Council
House of Lords Record Office, House of Lords Journals
Firth, C. H. (ed.), *Acts and Ordinances of the Interregnum* (London: HMSO, 1911)
Hill, G. W. and Frere, W. H., *Memorials of Stepney Parish – The Vestry Minutes from 1579 to 1662* (Guildford: Billing and Sons, 1890–91)
Parliamentary Archives, House of Commons Journals

Diaries
De Beer, E. S. (ed.), *The Diary of John Evelyn* (London: Everyman's Library, 2006)
Exwood, Maurice, and Lehmann, H. L. (eds.), *The Journal of William Schellinks' Travels in England 1661–1663* (London: Camden Society, 1993)
Latham, Robert, and Matthews, William (eds.), *The Diary of Samuel Pepys* (London: Bell & Hyman, 1970–74)

Journals, Pamphlets etc. (bound and unbound)
British Library
    Thomason Tracts, various, including: E99-(17), E99-(27), E104-(25), E202-(28), E400-(35), E445-(9, 10, 22, 26, 27, 42), E446-(11), E453-(37), E466-(32), E669-(5, 33)
    Additional Manuscripts
    Whitelocke, B., Annals, 37-343
    Malignauts Treacherous and Bloody Plot (18 August, 1643), BL Kings 669 f. 8 No. 22

Guildhall Library
    Carpenters' Company, Court Minutes, Manuscript 4329/5
    Fishmongers' Company, Index to Court Ledger, No. 3 (1631 to 1646), Manuscript 5572/3
    Fishmongers' Company, Court Minutes, Manuscript 5570/3
    Painters-Stainers' Company, Court Minutes, Manuscript 5667/1

Lambeth Archives
    The Accounts of Mr Robert White Mr Edward Smith and Ambrose Andrews, Churchwardens of the parish of Lambeth for this yeere Ann' Dom'i 1644

National Archives, Kew
    SP19, Pt 1
    SP24/11
    SP24/36SP24/58
    SP28/139 Pt 10

BIBLIOGRAPHY

Carter, Matthew, *A True relation of that honourable, though unfortunate expedition of Kent, Essex and Colchester in 1648* (Colchester: J. Marsden, 1810)

Mercurius Aulicus, ending 29 June. 1644, Oxford, 1644

Mercurius Civicus, 4 May 1643 to 26 December 1644 (Reading: Tyger's Head Books, 2013–14) 2 Volumes

Perfect Diurnall of Some Passages in Parliament (May 1643)

A True and Perfect Relation of the Barbarous and Cruell Passages of The Kings Army, At Old-Brainceford, Neer London, Thomason Tract (reprinted in Chippendale, Neil, *The Battle of Brentford* (Leigh-on-Sea: Partizan Press, 1991)

Husband (ed.), *A Collection Of all the publicke Orders, Ordinances and Declarations of both Houses of Parliament, from the Ninth of March 1642 until December 1646*, T. W., London (1646)

Lithgow, William, *The Present Surveigh At London* (1643). Reprinted in Ross, W. G., *Military Engineering during the Great Civil War, 1642–9* (London: Ken Trotman / Lionel Leventhal Limited, 1984)

Varley, F. J. (ed.), *Mercurius Aulicus – A Diurnall Communicating the Intelligence and Affaires of the Court to the Rest of the Kingdome* (Oxford: Basil Blackwell, 1948)

Books

Hobbes, Thomas, *Behemoth, or the Long Parliament* (Chicago: University of Chicago Press, 1990)

Hyde, Edward Earl of Clarenedon, *The History of the Great Rebellion* (Oxford: Oxford University Press, 1826)

Stow, John, *A Survey of London* (Stroud: The History Press, 2005)

Vicar, John, *England's Worthies under whom all the Civil and Bloudy Warres since Anno 1642 to Anno 1647* (London, 1647)

Secondary Sources

Books

Barry, J. (ed.), *The Tudor and Stuart Town, 1530–1688: A Reader in English Urban History* (Harlow: Longman Group UK Limited, 1990)

Besant, W., *London in the Time of the Stuarts* (London: Adam and Charles Black, 1903)

Beier, A. L. and Finlay, R. (eds.), *London 1500–1700, The Making of the Metropolis* (Harlow: Longman Group Limited, 1986)

Blackmore, David, *Arms and Armour of the English Civil War* (London: Royal Armouries, 1990)

Brett-James, Norman G., *The Growth of Stuart London* (London: George Allen and Unwin Limited, 1935)

Carlton, Charles, *Going to the Wars* (London: BCA, 1992)

Chippendale, Neil, *The Battle of Brentford* (Leigh-on-Sea: Partizan Press, 1991)

Cocroft, Wayne D., *Dangerous Energy* (Swindon: English Heritage, 2000)

Edwards, Peter, *Dealing in Death: The Arms Trade and the British Civil Wars, 1638–52* (Stroud: Sutton Publishing Limited, 2000)

Ellis, John, *To Walk in the Dark: Military Intelligence during the English Civil War* (Stroud: The History Press, 2011)

Emberton, Wilfrid, *Skippon's Brave Boys* (Buckingham: Quotes Limited, 1984)

Everitt, Alan, *The Community of Kent and the Great Rebellion 1640–60* (Leicester: Leicester University Press, 1986)

Ffoulkes, Charles, *The Gun-Founders of England* (London: Arms and Armour Press, 1969)

Finlay, R., *Population and Metropolis – The Demography of London, 1580–1650* (Cambridge: Cambridge University Press, 1981)

Flintham, David, *London in the Civil War* (Leigh-on-Sea: Partizan Press, 2008)

Flintham, David, *The English Civil War Defences of London* (Bristol: Stuart Press, 2014)

Gardiner, S. R., *History of the Great Civil War* (Adlestrop: The Windrush Press, 1987)

Gardiner, S. R., *History of the Commonwealth and Protectorate* (Adlestrop: The Windrush Press, 1988)

Gaunt, Peter, *The Cromwellian Gazetteer* (Gloucester: Alan Sutton Publishing, 1987)

Gerhold, Dorian, *The Putney Debates, 1647* (Putney: Dorian Gerhold, 2007)

Grimes, W. F., *The Excavation of Roman and Mediaeval London* (London: Routledge & Kegan Paul PLC, 1968)

Harris, Tim, *London Crowds in the Reign of Charles II* (Cambridge: Cambridge University Press, 1990)

Haslam, R. and Ridgeway, V., *Excavations at the British Museum: An Archaeological and Social History of Bloomsbury*, British Museum Research Publication 210 (London: British Museum Press, 2017)

Herbert, W., *The History of the Twelve Great Livery Companies of London* (London: William Herbert, 1836)

Johnson, D. J., *Southwark and the City* (Oxford: Oxford University Press, 1969)

Jones, Nigel, *Tower* (London: Windmill Books, 2011)

Kenyon, John, and Ohlmeyer, Jane (eds.), *The Civil Wars: A Military History of England, Scotland and Ireland, 1638–60* (Oxford: Oxford University Press, 1998)

Lindley, K., *Popular Politics and Religion in Civil War London* (Aldershot: Scholar Press, 1997)

Manning, Brian, *The English People and the English Revolution* (London: Bookmarks, 1991)

Milward, R. J., *Wimbledon in the Time of the Civil War* (Epsom: Woodcote Publications Limited, 1976)

Monteth, Robert, *The History of the Troubles of Great Britain* (London: A. Millar, 1738)

Parry, Graham, *Hollar's England* (Salisbury: Michael Russell, 1980)

Pearl, Valerie, *London and the Outbreak of the Puritan Revolution, City Government and National Politics, 1625–43* (Oxford: Oxford University Press, 1961)

Picard, Liza, *Elizabeth's London* (London: W&N, 2004)

Picard, Liza, *Restoration London* (London: W&N, 2004)

Plowden, Alison, *In a Free Republic: Life in Cromwell's England* (Stroud: The History Press, 2006)

Porter Stephen (ed.), *London and the Civil War* (Basingstoke: Macmillan Press Limited, 1996)

Porter, Stephen, *The Plagues of London* (Stroud: Tempus, 2008)

Porter, Stephen, *Pepys' London: Everyday Life in London, 1650–1703* (Stroud: Amberly, 2011)

Porter, Stephen, *The Blast of War – Destruction in the English Civil Wars* (Stroud: The History Press, 2011)

Porter, Stephen, and Marsh, Simon, *The Battle for London* (Stroud: Amberly, 2011)

Rees, John, *The Leveller Revolution* (London: Verso, 2016)

Reese, Peter, *The Life of General George Monck* (Barnsley: Pen and Sword Books Limited, 2008)

Roberts, Keith, *London and Liberty* (Leigh-on-Sea: Partizan Press, 1987)

Roberts, Keith, *Cromwell's War Machine* (Barnsley: Pen and Sword Books Limited, 2013)

Ross, Lieutenant-Colonel W. G., R. E., *Military Engineering during the Great Civil War, 1642–9* (London: Ken Trotman / Lionel Leventhal Limited, 1984)

Rushworth, J., *Historical Collections* (1721)

Sharpe, R. R., *London and the Kingdom* (London: Longmans, Green and Co., 1894)

Stuckley, William, British Coins (London, 1776)

Tindall, Gillian, *The Man Who Drew London* (London: Pimlico, 2003)

Tinniswood, Adrian, *The Rainborowes* (London: Vintage Books, 2014)

Tomalin, Clare, *Samuel Pepys: The Unequalled Self* (London: Penguin Books Limited, 2012)

BIBLIOGRAPHY

Urban, Mark, *Generals: Ten British Commanders Who Shaped the World* (London: Faber and Faber Limited, 2006)
Weinstein, Rosemary, *Tudor London* (London: HMSO, 1994)
Wynn-Jones, Robert, *The Lost City of London* (Stroud: Amberley, 2012)

Journals
Arms & Armour Society
The Journal of the Arms & Armour Society, vol. VI, no. 3, September 1968

Fortress Study Group
Fort, Volume 25 (1997)

London Archaeologist
The London Archaeologist
  Volume 2, No. 13 (Winter 1975)
  Volume 8, supplement 1 (1996)
  Volume 8, No. 9 (Summer 1998)

London and Middlesex Archaeological Society
Transactions 35 (1984)

London Topographical Society
London Topographical Record
  Volume 14 (1928)
  Volume 45 (1997)

Maps
Hyde, Ralph (ed.), *The A to Z of Georgian London* (London: London Topographical Society, 1981)
Hyde, Ralph (ed.), *The A to Z of Restoration London, 1676* (London: London Topographical Society, 1992)
Prockter, Adrian and Taylor, Robert (eds.), *The A to Z of Elizabethan London* (London: London Topographical Society, 1979)
Saunders, Ann (ed.), *The A to Z of Charles II's London, 1682* (London: London Topographical Society, 2013)
Vertue, George, 'Plan of the City of London as fortified by Order of Parliament in the years 1642 and 1643' (1738), Amended by Cromwell Mortimer M.D. in 1746, Kings Topographical Collection, Vol. XX, No. 16.

Unpublished Works
Schroeder, John Juergen, *London and the Civil Wars* (University of Wisconsin, 1954)

Other
Archives for London Conference: *Parliamentary Hospitals in London during the Civil Wars and Interregnum* (London: London Metropolitan Archives, 4 October 2008)
University of Leicester, *'Battle-Scarred', Surgery, Medicine and Military Welfare during the British Civil Wars* (Leicester: University of Leicester, 2016)